The God-Kings
of
the Vikings

The Viking Dynasties and their Conquests of Northern Europe
(850-1086)

by Hugh Montgomery

THE BOOK TREE
San Diego, California

ISBN 978-1-58509-124-9

Cover layout
Atulya Berube

Interior layout & design
Atulya Berube

Front Cover: A medieval Norse stronghold
inset with 17th century portrait of William I
based upon contemporary records.

Published by
The Book Tree
P O Box 16476
San Diego, CA 92176
www.thebooktree.com

We provide fascinating and educational products to help awaken the public to new ideas and information that would not be available otherwise.
Call 1 (800) 700-8733 for our *FREE BOOK TREE CATALOG*.

Contents

List of Figures

Photos

Ulvungar

The concept of the Ulvungar Dynasty was first used by the late Bo-Gabriel Montgomery in his book *Ancient Migrations and Royal Families*. It was further enlarged upon by the author with the permission of the estate of the Bo-Gabriel. The Terms *Ulvungar* and *Ulvungar Dynasty* are copyright to the estate and the author severally and jointly and may not be used unless reference is made to the copyright owners. The Ulvungar Dynasty identifies those who are reasonably shown to be descendants, male or female, of Ataulf and Maria.

In *Puck of Pook's Hill* by Rudyard Kipling there is a poem called *Song of the Fifth River*, which inspired me to write the following, but whilst Kipling's river is a river of gold, this river is a bloodline.

*Uôuin's River

Four rivers flowed out of Eden,
Or so the legends tell,
But there was a fifth and hidden one,
A river of blood, as well.

The four rivers meandered outwards,
As from Eden they went forth.
All of the globe they covered,
East, West, South and North.

The fifth river was a bloodline,
Of a noble and royal race
And the fifth river ruled all the others,
Though in its own time and place.

Many were priests, kings and cohens,
And noble warriors too
All stemmed from this fifth river,
All kept the bloodline true.

Babylon, Israel and Egypt,
These kingdoms were not alone,
For Goths, Vikings and Romans,
All bowed down to *Uôuin's throne.

(* Pronounced Euen (Ewen) = Odin)

INTRODUCTION

In my trilogy of books, *The God-Kings of Europe, The God-Kings of England* and *The God-Kings of Outremer*, I outlined the story of the great Scandinavian and Visigothic Ulvungar family. However it has become apparent through discussions with on-line forums and with individuals that there were gaps in between the three books which needed filling. This book is an updated version and replacement of *The God-Kings of England*, now out of print, and is intended to fill in all the gaps between these books that were previously left out. It incorporates parts of all three books and in particular book two, but includes some information that was deliberately left out or new information that has become available since.

In my previous book *The God Kings of Europe* I showed how the early Christian/Judaic Church had been suborned by the Roman Empire. How they had agreed to write Jesus' descendents and family out of history. How they took from them the family Bishoprics of Jerusalem, Alexandria, Antioch and Ephesus. And how one Church Father actually proclaimed that Jesus had been preaching the wrong religion!

The Church would have succeeded had not a descendant of Jesus himself, Maria of the Elchasaites, married the King of the Visigoths, Ataulf. This marriage to the Conquerors of Rome allowed the families of Jesus and his brethren to continue under their protection and formed the basis for the great Ulvungar dynasty, descended from Herioldus Brocus or Lothbroc. The Ulvungars bided their time but eventually counter-attacked. They launched Viking raids into both Europe and England and then decided on a policy of occupation, first in Normandy, where one branch became the Dukes of Normandy and later Kings of England. The family was to be kept safe but undercover, accepting the hated Baptism if that is what it took, but keeping alive their ancient Mesopotamian and Middle Eastern origins. I will be showing some important DNA evidence during the course of this book.

Most people think of the Viking and Danish occupations of England as completely divorced from the Conquest of Normandy, but as this book will show, the Norman Conquest of England was merely one of the successful invasions by the Ulvungar Dynasty. The Conquest of England was planned and started by the Ulvungars many years before and completed by their descendants. The Conquest of Normandy was started by Godfrid and Sigfrid and completed by Rollo Keitel's son and Roger Gorm's son, and the Norman conquest of England was planned and executed by five men, their descendants:

William of Duke of Normandy, Robert de Beaumont, Roger de Montgomery, Robert d'Eu and William Fitz-Osbern, all Ulvungar descendants.

But the Conquest of England would not have been possible without the information gleaned from the Conquest of Sicily, as explained in *The God-Kings of Outremer*, and that too was planned and executed by members and cousins of the House of Normandy. Without the experience so gained, the first crusade would not have been the only successful crusade made by western forces.

Chapter 1

Yet, when the signs of summer thicken,
And the ice breaks, and the birch-buds quicken,
Yearly you turn from our side, and sicken–

Sicken again for the shouts and slaughters,
You steal away to the lapping waters,
And look at your ship in her winter quarters.

(From the Harp song of the Dane women – *Puck of Pook's Hill* by Rudyard Kipling)

The Beginnings of Normandy

In 881 Louis of France had successfully defeated the combined armies of the Vikings in Gaul at the sanguinary battle of Saultcourt. The French and their monarch must have supposed that they would at the very least have bought themselves and the rest of northern Europe some breathing space from Viking/Norse expeditions, which had been going on since Charlemagne's time. These expeditions, which in many cases were more than merely raids for booty, had been launched to a very large extent to interrupt the hegemony of the new Roman Empire, which had sprung up to replace the old Empire, against which the Gothic Norse had fought for so long. In fact, Herioldus Brocus or Hylthetan, who was king of most of Denmark, was killed whilst preparing a major expedition to overthrow Charlemagne.[1] It is probable that it was Herioldus who planned to extend his kingdom to include northern France, in what became Normandy, all of England and possibly Ireland as well. For example, the two sons of Godfrid, king of Westfold, each became king of Dublin one after another. In the Irish annals they are called Amhlaeibh and Imhar.[1a]

But already in November of that year, 881, a new force of Norsemen moved up the Meuse and took up winter quarters at Haslou or Eslo.[1b] This group was led by the Princes Sigfrid and Godfrid, though they are both styled as Kings in the Chronicles. Sigfrid was the son of Hemming, King of Denmark.[2]

Godfrid was his nephew, the son of Harald, King of South Jutland. Sigfrid had with him his son Gorm (Wurm) and his brother Halfdan.[3] Their winter quarters were not far from Maastricht and were in the form of a fortified camp made from earthenworks thrown up with sharpened halftrunks of trees on top. Within this outer perimeter they built temporary, long houses for the winter.

In the summer of 882 this group proceeded to raid the countryside round about. They seized the towns of Maastricht, Liege, Coblenz, Cologne and Bonn, as well as the surrounding countryside. In Aachen they turned the Imperial Palace into a stable for their horses, whilst other imperial castles such as Zilpich, Jülich and Nuys were burnt to the ground. The rich monasteries of Pruym, Stablo and Malmedy were plundered of their treasures and then set alight.

Faced with this major invasion, the "Holy" Roman Emperor, Charles-le-Gros, raised a large army and besieged the Norse in their camp at Eslo. Sigfrid and Godfrid however did not attempt to fight. Instead they parlayed. In return for a large Danegeld in gold and silver amounting to some two thousand pounds (a huge amount in those days), they agreed to leave imperial territory, though not mainland Europe itself. Additionally, Godfrid obtained all of Friezeland, as Count of Friezeland, from the mouth of the Weser in the North to the mouth of the Scheldt in the South. Interestingly enough, according to the Annals of Fulda, this was bestowed as allodial land, suggesting that Godfrid could claim this as lands previously owned by his family.[4] Godfrid and Sigfrid agreed to be baptised and at some stage, probably later, the Emperor bestowed upon Godfrid, Gisella, daughter of the late King Lothair of Lorraine.

In 885 Godfrid fell into a trap set by the Emperor, the Bishop of Cologne, and the Counts of Saxon-Thüringen and Friuli, Henry and Everard, respectively. Godfrid agreed to come to a feast with his wife and only a few followers. The Bishop of Cologne had persuaded Gisella to leave him or possibly to betray him at the feast, and Godfrid and his men were cut down. After this murder Sigfrid became the leader of all the Norse in both Friezeland and France, and besieged Paris in 885. He returned to Friezeland at the end of 885 but was killed in 887. Sigfrid's son Gorm, meanwhile returned to England, taking with him much of the booty obtained by his father, and where he became king of Northumberland. He was known as Gorm-hin-ricke (or Gorm the rich), presumably from the amount of booty he brought back with him. He should not be confused with Gorm (alias Guthrum), who became king of East-Anglia. They are both styled as Danish kings but in fact were second cousins who ruled over different parts of England. Gorm-hin-ricke was also known sometimes as Gormeric (or Little Gorm), to distnguish him from Guthrum of East-Anglia.

Gorm of Northumberland was killed in 894, but his son Ragnar Gormsson returned to France and established himself in what is now lower Normandy, near to Exmes, where he built a Motte and Bailey Castle on a small hill. This was a wooden palisade and earthen worked ditch, within which a wooden house or bailey stronghold was built. It is entirely possible that this had been built earlier by his father, but at all events he called it the Hill of Gormeric or Gormerici and it became known as Mons Go(r)merici. Ragnar either accepted baptism or had already been baptised at the court of his father. I personally think that he accepted baptism in France at the same time that he was given the title of Count of Exmes, taking the name Roger or Rogerius as his Christian name. At all events, by 905 in the Charter of Pitres he is called Rogerius Mons Gomerici Comes Exmesis (Roger of Mount Gomeri, Count of Exmes). (5)

The remains of Mons Gomerici today

There exists a document in the Bibliotheque Nationale in Paris,[6] which states that the 1st Count Roger de Montgomery accompanied Duke Roul (Rollo) in his conquest of Neustria in 885. I believe, however, that the copiest has made an error with the date, which he has put down as 885 when it should be 895, otherwise the name of the duke would have been Sigfroi.[7] As we shall see in a minute, the date of 895 for this document is confirmed by other chronicles of the period.

In the late summer of 895, five Viking longboats entered the mouth of the Seine and moved up towards Rouen. The leader of this expedition was called Rollo,[8] though as we shall see he had various names, not least of which was Hunedanus.[9] Near to Rouen they halted and made camp to await reinforcements. Both the *Chron. de Gestis Normanorum*[10] and the *Annales Vesdatine*[11] make clear that Rollo received reinforcements ("with numbers increased"), but neither of them, nor the *Chron. Rerum Septrionalium*, which also mentions the events, but calls the leader Rodo, indicates from where these reinforcements came. However, if we now go back to the French Manuscript mentioned earlier[5&6] then it is fairly obvious that the reinforcements were provided by Rollo's fourth cousin Ragnar Gormsson or Rogerius de Mons Gomerici, as he became known in Latin, or Roger de Montgomery in French, and who indeed became the first Montgomery Count, as the manuscript calls him, as Count of Exmes, just as Rollo was to become Count of Rouen.

This was, however, not the first time that Rollo had been part of an expedition to France. According to English chroniclers Odericus Vitalis and Florence of Worcester, "Rollo and his followers landed in Normandy on the fifteenth of the calends of Dec. (17th November) 876."[12] He and his father Keitel also appear to have been part of the forces under Sigfrid who besieged Paris in 885. Indeed, after Sigfrid's death Keitel (also known as Oscetil) and Rollo appear to have operated on their own, based on the isle of Oscelle, which may well have been named after Oscetil.[13] Eventually, their forces were defeated by Eudes (Odo) in 888 at Montfaucon. Keitel appears to disappear from the campaign at this point, but if he escaped he almost certainly returned to Russia from whence he had come on the expedition (see Appendix under Keitel's son).

Let us return now to the campaign of 895. This too ended in defeat for Rollo or, at the very least a stalemate, and he agreed to settle in Neustria and was baptised in 896, "Charles raised up Huncdeus from the font."[14] It is likely that Hunedanus was given his first Christian name of Rollo at this point, but he returned to his Odonic beliefs later and had to be baptised a second time in 912, when he was given the second Christian name of Robert, Count of Rouen at the treaty of St. Clair-sur-Epte.

This then was the real beginning of the Dukedom of Normandy with Rollo, now Robert, based in Rouen in the north and his fourth cousin Ragnar, now Roger, based in Lower Normandy at Exmes. Later, still, the descendants of these two would combine to conquer England, though on many occasions the rivalry between the Ducal House and the Montgomerys turned murderous.

It had been assumed by historians for many years that the Dukedom of Normandy had been formed by the grants made to Rollo in 911/12 and by further grants to his successor William Longsword, by King Rudolf in 924 and 933, respectively. However, I, and many others, now think that Normandy was formed more by Norman force of arms and expansionist ideas and that the grants merely constituted a situation that existed *de facto*.[15] Certainly Normandy took shape principally under the sixteen-year reign of William Longsword and the even longer fifty-two year reign of Count later Duke Richard I. To Richard must be given the credit for the marriage alliances he forged through his second wife Gunnora and her sisters Weva and Senfrie, which helped cement and stabilise the Norman aristocracy under his control. By the end of his reign, Normandy was very much as William the Conqueror inherited it.

It is another member of the Montgomery kin who must take credit for helping Count William (he was not yet styled Duke) and later protecting the young Count Richard. He is known to history as Bernard the Dane and was born circa 880. At the beginning of the 930s he put down a serious revolt by another Norman/Viking, Riouf, who had a power base in the west and had besieged the Count in Rouen. In 935 he put down a further major revolt in the Bessin and Cotentin by Viking communities who had not accepted William's authority.

Upon William's death by assassination, Bernard, together with Anslech de Bricquebec, Osmond de Conteville and Raoul Taisson, became a Regent for the Duchy and when the French king Louis and Hugh the Great, Duke of the Franks attacked, Bernard appealed to Harald Bluetooth and his Danes to help defend the Duchy. The document previously cited (5 & 6) makes clear that Bernard and William de Montgomery both descend from the first Roger de Montgomery, though it is not clear if William was Bernard's brother or his nephew. On the basis of dates, I have made William de Montgomery, Bernard's brother (App. VIII), but frankly either could be correct. From Bernard it is believed descend two great Anglo-Norman families – the Beaumonts and the Harcourts.[16]

What is interesting is that although the Vikings had caused a considerable amount of havoc over a period of some two hundred years, they were always eventually beaten in a stand up battle with the French. The French were already using the "horsed-knight" against which, on open ground, the Norse/Vikings could not stand. But the Vikings controlled the coasts and the rivers and waterways with their longboats. It was this combination of control of the seas and rivers, which together with the mailed horsemen, would make the new Norse or Normans so formidable, it would allow them to conquer northern France, England, southern Italy and Outremer.

References Chapter 1

1,1a &1b – see Appendix II.

2. "Siwarth Hemmingnag Sun" – *Series Runica Prima.*

3. Contracted Hals or Half, short for Halfdanus in the Chronicles.

4. Reuter, T. (Translator)(1992) - *Annales of Fulda*, p. 143, Mancheter University Press.

5. Charter of Pitres quoted in Montgomery, H. (2002) – *The Montgomery Millennium*, Megatrend, Belgrade & London.

6. *Ms. Français 20780*, cabinet des titres 20.780, fols. 221-23, Bibliotheque Nationale, Paris.

7. "Roger Gommer I du nom fit bastir la ma(aison) de son surnom… Il fut le premier comte de Montgomery et l'un des princes qui accompagnerent le Duc Roul (otherwise should be Sigfroi) a la conqueste de Neustrie environ l'an 885." A more complete form of this document is quoted in Appendix II.

8. *Chron. de Gestis Normanorum in Francia* A. D. 895 (edition Duchesne), "The Northman again with their duke who is named Rollo, entered the Seine, and before Christmas moved up the Oise with their numbers increased."

9. *Annals Vedastine* for 895-896, "At the same time the Northmen with their Duke whose name was Hunedeus (A slight misspelling) with five barges (longships) entered the seine… The Northman with increased numbers entered the Oise shortly before Christmas."

10. See note 8 above.

11. See note 9 above.

12. *The Chronicle of Florence of Worcester* for 876-877 (Trans. Forester, T.), (ed.1884) Henry Bohn, London.

13. For full details of this expedition, see Appendix IV (Keitel's son).

14. *Annals Vedastine* for 896. Note the same spelling as used for the leader of the Vikings previously.

15. Brown, R. A. (1984) – *The Normans*, p. 17 & footnotes, The Boydell Press.

16. Translation from the French document *Bernard le Danois* and quoted in:
http://en.wikipedia.org/wiki/Bernard_the_Dane

Chapter II

Howso great man's strength be reckoned,
There are two things he cannot flee;
Love is the first, and Death is the second –
And love, in England, hath taken me!

(From Sir Richard's song – *Puck of Pook's Hill* by Rudyard Kipling)

England and the Events that Lead to the Invasions

On a cold day in January 1066, probably on 5th, King Edward, known as "The Confessor", died. His death triggered events that have echoed down the ages. It marked the end of the reign of the Anglo-Saxon Royal line. It precipitated a series of events leading to the Norman Invasion and the replacement of the Anglo-Saxon Kings by the Norse line of the Dukes of Normandy and the Anglo-Saxon Thegns by the Norman Barons.

The reasons, however, go back over many years, and before we can judge the rights or wrongs involved or even why those events triggered the Invasion, it is first necessary to look at England and Europe for about 100 years or so before the events of 1066 and to look at the legal claims to the throne.

There may well be a case for saying that England, as a united kingdom, did not exist prior to the Norman Invasion. Certainly the Anglo-Saxons had pushed the native Celts back to the fringes of Britain, to what we would now call Scotland, Wales and Cornwall. Though it must be emphasised that the Celts were not themselves the original inhabitants and indeed should perhaps be called Romano-Celts, because recent archaeology suggests that they may well have been the last remnants of the old Western Roman Empire and indeed had maintained contact and trade with the Eastern Roman Empire in Byzantium after the fall of Rome itself, much longer that previously thought.[1]

They had conquered earlier inhabitants, before themselves being driven out to the fringes by the Anglo-Saxons.

There was however another group, who had already made their presence felt, and this was the Danes or Vikings and who together with the settled Vikings in Normandy were quite often referred to collectively as the "Norse or Norsemen." One of the curious things about modern historians is the belief that the Anglo-Saxons equal and were the same as the English. This may be politically correct but in reality the Anglo-Saxons were merely one of a group of people competing to be the dominant race in Albion (the ancient and at that time more traditional name for England – meaning the White Land – probably deriving from the sight of the white cliffs of Dover). Indeed, in my opinion it was the Danes who were the dominant race and not the Anglo-Saxons.

Prof. R. Allen Brown in his excellent book The Normans even suggests that the people of England, at the time of and just prior to the conquest, should be called Anglo-Scandinavians, rather than Anglo-Saxons. Certainly the Kingdoms of both Mercia and Northumbria were under Danelaw until at least 1042 and it could be argued that Wessex and East Anglia were merely subsidiary kingdoms owing allegiance to the Danish Crown. In fact, the House of Wessex, (West Saxons) and the one remaining Anglo-Saxon Kingdom in the year 900, only claimed to be "Kings of England" or possibly only "Kings of the English," as late as 937, with the defeat of the Scots and Norse army at Brunanburgh (probably near Rotherham in Yorkshire).[2]

In my book *The God Kings of Europe* I showed how the mighty Ulvungar dynasty was descended from the Visigothic and Davidic Royal Houses and how they had taken on and defeated the old Western Roman Empire and established a series of Kingdoms spanning most of France, Scandinavia and Russia. They had temporarily been pushed back by the Christianisation of Europe and the rise of the Charlemagnic dynasty backed by the Roman Catholic Church, but by the 9th century were back trying to recover their lands. The conquest of Normandy and England were to be vital in their designs.

In fig. 1, I have given a list of the rival Royal Houses of the Danes and Anglo-Saxons, which makes interesting reading. As can immediately be seen, at the same time as Aethelred II (known as The Unready) was supposed to be King, the Dane Sweyn Forkbeard seems to have been under the impression that he was King of England.

Fig. 1 - Kings of England 980 - 1066

Anglo-Saxon	Danes
Aethelred II (978 - 1016)	Sweyn Forkbeard (983 - 1014)
Edmund Ironside (1014 - 1016)	Cnut (Canute) (1014 - 1035)
Edward the Exile (1016 - 1042) d. 1057	Harold Harefoot (1035 - 1040)
Edward the Confessor (1042 - 1066)	Harthacnut (1040 - 1042)

Norwegian

Magnus (1042 until his death)	Sweyn Esthrithson (1042 - 1066 but continued to claim)

(Source for Danish Line - *Den Store Danske Encyklopaedi*, 1998 Edition)

Aethelred had killed his elder brother Eadweard II (known afterwards as Edward the Martyr) in 978 and usurped the throne. He was known throughout his life as "The Unready" or more properly as "Unraed," meaning evil counsel, almost certainly as an ironic twist to his name Aethelred, which means "Noble Counsel."[3]

The House of Wessex, which became the Anglo-Saxon Royal House, were probably descended from the Visigoth King, Rhoes theWeoôulgeot (or Odin-God), as set out in my book *The God-Kings of Europe*. The Wessex King List, which shows descent from Odin, almost certainly in reality shows descent from Rhoes the Odin rather than the mythical God figure (see Appendix 16).

Meanwhile, Sweyn Forkbeard arrived in England with a large army and deposed Aethelred in 1013 and proclaimed himself, King of England by conquest. Sweyn was the son of Harold Bluetooth and grandson of Gorm the Old, King of Denmark[4] and consequently an Ulvungar. In fact, Gorm his grandfather was second cousin to Hrolf or Rollo, founder of the Norman Dynasty (see Genealogy III). Sweyn's battle flag was that of the Black Raven, the Norse bird of battle and victory, to be seen on many a hard fought battle scene, pecking out the eyes of the fallen. A much later battle, that of Kossovo in Serbia, is known as the Field of Blackbirds, but more properly in English should be called the Field of Ravens.

Sweyn died in 1014 and was buried at Lincoln, but Aethelred had had enough and fled to Normandy, to the safety of his wife's family and abdicated, dying there in 1016. Again it is usual to talk of Aethelred paying large amounts of "Danegeld" to keep the Danes at bay, but the Danes saw this rather differently. So far as they were concerned this was simply taxes, which the subject Anglo-Saxons owed to them, their overlords. What we must appreciate is that the Danes had considered for generations that the north of England was theirs (the Kingdoms of Northumbria and Mercia) and even today this North-South divide still exists. For much of this time too, the Scots allied themselves with the Norse against the Anglo-Saxons. The very Scots word for a foreigner is Sassanach, meaning Saxon.

Meanwhile, Aethelred's son, Edmund Ironside, took the opportunity with the death of Sweyn to seize his father's throne, coming to England in 1014 and proclaiming himself King. His assumption of the throne did not last long, however, for with the arrival in England of Cnut, the son of Sweyn and known to generations of school children as King Canute, he was forced into a deal. He could keep the old Anglo-Saxon Kingdom of Wessex as under-king to Cnut, but should one die, then whoever survived would become King of ALL ENGLAND. Unfortunately for Edmund it was he who died within a year, and Cnut who became King of All England.

Cnut reigned for 21 years and during this time England became very much Danish in outlook. The Roman Church lost much of its influence and polygamy became, if not commonplace, then at least not unusual – led by Cnut himself, who, although already married to Aelgifa of Northampton, took Emma (in Anglo-Saxon, "Aelgyfu"), the widow of Aethelred II, as his second wife; his first wife remaining in Denmark.

Some historians have called his first wife a mistress, but as with the case of Harold Hardrada, I believe the case for polygamy is overwhelming (see notes on Polygamy App. I). Emma, who was of the Ducal family of Normandy, and importantly for Cnut a member of the Ulvungar dynasty, was also great-aunt of William the Conqueror. She already had a son by Aethelred – Edward (later to be known as "The Confessor"). By Cnut she had at least two children, a son Harthacnut and a daughter Gunnhild.

Just to make life difficult for students of history, Aethelred had also been married before he married Emma, to a lady by the name of Elfreda, and which unfortunately also translates as Elgifu. In order to try to help the reader, I have used different spellings for each lady and have generally referred to Emma using her Norman name. By Elfreda, Aethelred had a son, Edmund Ironside, to whom we have already referred and who in turn had a son called Edward – known either as Edward the Atheling (which simply means heir) or Edward the Exile, as although the Anglo-Saxons regarded him as their king, he in fact never set foot in England until just before his death in 1057. (5) (See figs. 2 & 3 headed "Descendants of Cnut" and "Descendants of Aethelred II.")

Upon the death of Cnut his eldest son Sweyn, by Aelgifa of Northampton, became King of Norway and his son by Emma, Harthacnut, became King of both Denmark and England. However Cnut had a second son by Aelgifa called Harold Harefoot, who decided to try his luck in England. It is uncertain whether he was sent as his younger brother's deputy or whether he simply came to England of his own volition, but at all events he arrived in England shortly after Cnut's death and, finding his brother Harthacnut very unpopular with certain sections of the population, had himself crowned as King Harold I and reigned from 1035 until 1040. Emma, who apparently loathed Harefoot, together with her sons by Aethelred, Edward and Alfred, made an abortive invasion of England from Normandy, but were defeated by Harefoot who captured Alfred and had him blinded so badly that he died. Edward meanwhile, fled back to Normandy. (This question of blinding of liege lords is dealt with in some detail in *The God Kings of Europe*).

In 1040 Harthacnut got together a large force and arrived in England presuming that he was going to have to fight his elder brother for the throne of England, only to discover on landing that Harold Harefoot had died about two weeks previously. Harthacnut took his revenge by having his brother's body dug up and thrown into a bog.

Harthacnut was in this supported somewhat naturally by his mother, Emma, but he was nonetheless deeply unpopular with his Anglo-Saxon subjects and perhaps at his mother's suggestion, brought over his elder half-brother Edward as something like co-king, but I think principally as a sop to the Anglo-Saxons.

It is interesting to look at some of the English Charters from Harthacnut's reign, many of which exist in part or in fragments in the Royal State Archives in Denmark and whose chief archivist has so kindly made photocopies available to me. For example,

Document No: 467 – dated 8th June 1042 says:

**"Ego Harðacnut ...rex Anglorum eque totius Albionis ....
Harðacnut rex totius Bryttanniae, Aelfgyfu eiusdem regis mater"**
(I Harthacnut ...King of the Angles (English?) and of all Albion ....
Harthacnut King of all Britain, the King's mother herself Aelfgyfu (Emma)).
Again, document No: 468 also dated 8th June 1042 says:

**"Ego Hardacnut, Christo conferente, rex et primicerius
Anglorum atque Danorum .....Hardacnut rex, Aelfgiua
eiusdem regis mater, Eadward praedicti regis frater"**
(I Harthacnut, conferred by Christ, King and first of the Angles and Danes.....
Harthacnut King, Aelfgiua (Emma) herself mother of the King, Edward
aforementioned brother of the King).

It is clearly Harthacnut[6] who is King of England and not Edward, indeed there is no suggestion in any of these charters of "Eadward co-rex" or "etque Eadward rex."

It is equally clear that the Edward referred to is Edward the Confessor and not Edward the Exile, who at this point the Anglo-Saxons would like to think is King of England.

When Harthacnut died without legitimate heirs, his will divided his kingdoms up, making Magnus, King of Norway, his successor in England and Sweyn Esthrithson, a cousin, his heir to Denmark. Edward however was already in England and had brought with him a large number of Norman Knights and Barons, having lived for the first 25 years of his life in Normandy under the protection of the Norman Dukes, the last of whom was William the Conqueror. To William he had made the promise whilst still in Normandy that should he ever succeed to the Throne of England, then in the case of his death without children, William would become his heir. Edward therefore seized his opportunity and had himself crowned King of England. This act provoked outrage from Magnus, who wrote him a letter which still exists in which he makes it clear that Edward is merely his regent, ruling until such time as he, Magnus, comes to claim his throne.[7]

Edward was in fact very lucky. He replied to Magnus's letter that he, Edward, was the legal successor to Harthacnut.[8] Had Magnus not been preoccupied with Denmark and Norway it is likely that he would have invaded England to claim his throne and it is very likely that with the help of Harold Hardrada, his co-King, and the most famous warrior of his day, that he would have succeeded. In fact William's eventual success owes much to this dispute, as we shall see. One thing that is clear from all these claims is that, however much modern politically correct democrats may dislike the idea, it is quite plain that there was an assumption that a King could nominate his successor and that the land and its people went with that nomination, though quite often the people themselves objected and frequently opposed the nominee by force of arms. There is some dispute as to the position of the Witen or Witenagemot (Anglo-Saxon Council). Some historians maintain that the Witen had to approve the new King.[9] My only comment is that in that case the Danish royal line seems to have dispensed with this approval.

At this point it is worthwhile to look at the descendants of both Cnut and Aethelred, to see the family interrelationships and the various claims to the throne.

Fig. 2 - DESCENDANTS OF CNUT

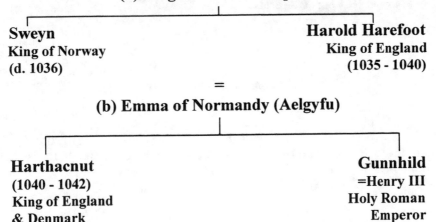

CNUT (1016 - 1035)
=
(a) Aelgifa of Northampton

Sweyn
King of Norway
(d. 1036)

Harold Harefoot
King of England
(1035 - 1040)
=
(b) Emma of Normandy (Aelgyfu)

Harthacnut
(1040 - 1042)
King of England
& Denmark

Gunnhild
=Henry III
Holy Roman
Emperor

Fig. 3 - DESCENDANTS OF AETHELRED

Aethelred II (Called the "Unraed")

=

(a) Elfreda (Elgifu)

|

Edmund Ironside
King of England (1014 - 1016)

|

Edward the Aethling (The Exile)
(d. 1057)
= Agatha (dau. King Stephen of Hungary)

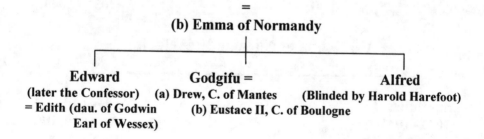

Margaret
(Later St. Margaret)
= Malcolm III King of the Scots

Edgar the Athling

=

(b) Emma of Normandy

Edward
(later the Confessor)
= Edith (dau. of Godwin
Earl of Wessex)

Godgifu =
(a) Drew, C. of Mantes
(b) Eustace II, C. of Boulogne

Alfred
(Blinded by Harold Harefoot)

Fig. 4 - DESCENDANTS OF RICHARD I COUNT OF NORMANDY

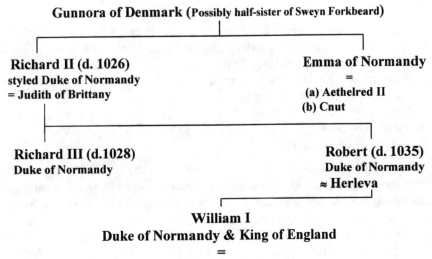

Richard I Count of Normandy (d. 996)

=

Gunnora of Denmark (Possibly half-sister of Sweyn Forkbeard)

Richard II (d. 1026)
styled Duke of Normandy
= Judith of Brittany

Emma of Normandy

=

(a) Aethelred II
(b) Cnut

Richard III (d.1028)
Duke of Normandy

Robert (d. 1035)
Duke of Normandy
≈ **Herleva**

William I
Duke of Normandy & King of England

=

Matilda of Flanders
(Descendant of Alfred the Great)

As we can see from fig. 2, Cnut had married twice, first to Aelgifa of Northampton by whom he had two sons, Sweyn, who became King of Norway and Harold Harefoot who, as we mentioned previously, became King of England from 1035 to 1040.

Secondly, he married Emma of Normandy, indeed he went so far as to demand she become his wife, though by all accounts Emma was not unhappy with this choice. I would suggest that he needed to marry back into the Ulvungar dynasty not only to protect his throne from incursions by this powerful younger branch of the family, but also to reinforce this "semi-divine" dynasty descended from the Odonic and Davidic lines (see *The God Kings of Europe*).

By Emma, Cnut had two children, Harthacnut, who followed his father as King of Denmark and eventually King of England as well, and Gunnhild, a daughter who married the Holy Roman Emperor, Henry III. This of course created the possibility that the Ulvungars themselves could assume the very title and position that their ancestors had fought against so hard. What sweet revenge, that the very Empire which had tried to write the line of Jesus and Odin out of history should, via the marriage of Gunnhild and Henry, find itself ruled over by their successors!

We have already dealt with the descendants of Aethelred and it only remains to mention Margaret, the daughter of Edward the exile, who, unfortunately having been brainwashed in her youth, brought Scotland under the Roman Church, as opposed to the earlier Celtic Church, and who was eventually made a Saint for her efforts. It meant of course that the Scots royal family now had a claim to the English throne through her. Margaret had originally intended to become a nun and founded a nunnery in Hungary. She had, as the sister of the King, asked for and received a bit of the "True Cross" from the part that was kept at Colchester. It had been sent there by the Empress, later St. Helen, who had "found" the cross of the crucifixion and had had it divided into four parts (see *The God Kings of Europe*, Chapter 1). This was known as "The Holy Rood" and it is from this piece of wood that the Palace of Holyrood takes its name.

Who were the people claiming the throne of England in 1066? Firstly William, Duke of Normandy, descended from Herioldus Brocus, Halfdan and Bjorn Ironside, overlord of Scandinavia, as well as Gunnora of Denmark.[10] He was the nearest blood relative of Emma, his great-aunt, queen to two Kings of England. Via his wife he could claim to be a legitimate heir of the House of Wessex, because his wife Matilda was descended from Alfred the Great. Was promised the throne by Edward, his cousin, during Edward's stay in Normandy.[11] Supported as he supposed by Harold Godwinsson with a solemn oath.[12] He even arranged to have the backing of Pope Alexander, and is given a papal banner to bear into battle as a sign of his legitimate claim. Lastly, he has an agreement with Sweyn Esthrithson.

Secondly we have Sweyn Esthrithson, another Ulvungar, descended from Sweyn Forkbeard.[13] His mother was Estrith, daughter of Cnut, and his father Ulf, Regent of Denmark under Cnut.[14] Was designated heir of Harthacnut in Denmark and now King of Denmark, though fighting Magnus and Harold Hardrada. In his eyes, he was also rightfully King of England, as England was a vassal kingdom to Denmark. Was also promised the throne by Edward,[15] and the second person so promised, but in his case, "Even if Edward has children of his own." As we can see, King Edward's promises seem to mean little – no wonder he was called "The Confessor," he must have had a lot to confess!

Thirdly, there is the claim of Magnus of Norway. He was the designated heir of Harthacnut and accordingly, was the true King of England and not Edward. Perhaps that's why Edward did not seem to mind to whom he promised the throne? Magnus was supported by Emma against her own son, Edward. On his death his claim is taken up by Harold Hardrada, his co-king and uncle.

Fourthly, there was the claim by Harold Godwinsson, who had himself crowned King on Edward's death. He was the son of Gytha, sister of Ulf of Denmark, and therefore son-in-law of Cnut, and via his mother, an Ulvungar (see Appendix 5). His sister Edith had married King Edward, though they had no children and he had possibly been promised the throne by Edward on his deathbed. Certainly the Bayeaux Tapestry suggests this. Well what's one more, when you have already promised your throne to two other men!

There was also a faction at Edward's court who thought that the rightful heir was none of these but Walter, Count of the Vexin. Or if Eustace of Boulogne and Godgifu should have a daughter who then married, then her husband would have a right. It is interesting that Eustace made a trip to England in 1051 and although he was supposed to be an envoy for William, there are those who say that he was actively trying to get his own family declared heirs to the throne.[16] Certainly William remained extremely suspicious of Eustace's motives right up to the point he was crowned.

Amongst all of these claimants it is easy to forget the Anglo-Saxon claim, in the person of Edgar the Aethling (see fig. 3), who was in England at this time. According to Hungarian sources, Edgar and his sister Margaret were attempting to return to Hungary when their boat was forced, during a storm, to put in to port in Scotland and Margaret met Malcolm, whom she later married. Their mother was Agatha, daughter of King Stephen of Hungary, and they had been brought up in Hungary.[17]

William sends notice to Harold Godwinsson upon Edward's death, making his claim and reminding Harold of his oath to support William's claim. Harold, who has already been crowned, rejects his claim. William therefore prepares to invade and sets the date for August. Meanwhile, he sends Tostig to Harold Hardrada, now sole King of Norway after the death of Magnus, who takes up Magnus's claim and who also prepares to invade, together with Tostig, brother to Harold Godwinsson, now "King Harold." It is worthwhile to look at this it some detail. Tostig, himself an Ulvungar via his mother, was married to Judith, the aunt of William of Normandy. Tostig had been disinherited from his northern Earldom by his own brother and came over to Normandy to seek William's help. William sent him to Harald Hardrada, via Flanders, and I believe suggested a dual invasion with Harald landing in the North and William in the South of England, thus forcing the Anglo-Saxons to split their forces. What was the deal behind this? I don't know and unfortunately we shall never know for certain, but I suspect that William would have let Harald re-establish the old Danish Kingdom of York in the North, whilst William became King of the rest. Maybe William would even have been prepared to make England an under-Kingdom to Denmark. It certainly makes sense, as there was very little certainty that William's invasion would succeed on its own. Remember, Harald Hardrada had married into the Ulvungar dynasty and his children by Elizabeth could claim descent from Herioldus Brocus and Halfdan (see *The God Kings of Europe*, Chapter 9).

Bayeaux Tapestry Photo 1

Edward sends Harold to Normandy

References: Chapter 2

1. Brown, D. (2000) – *Ring gives Clue to Last Romans*, British Archaeology Journal, Journal of Council of British Archaeology, quoted in Daily Telegraph 25/4/00.

2. Dennys, R. CVO; OBE; FSA; Arundel Herald of Arms, (1987) – *Aethelstan in Our Royal Sovereigns*, Danbury, Surrey, UK. See also James, Edward (1988) – *The Northern World in the Dark Ages 400-900*, in The Oxford Illustrated History of Medieval Europe, Holmes, G. (ed.), Oxford, UK.

3. Dennys, R. op. cit. – *Aethelred II.*

4. Dennys, R. op.cit. – *Sweyn*. See also The New Encyclopaedia Britannica (1998), 15th Edition.

5. Bradbury, J. (1998) – *The Battle of Hastings*, p. 115, Sutton Publishing Ltd., Gloucestershire, UK.

6. *Den Store Danske Encyklopaedi* (1998) – See also Royal Danish Archives, Documents Nos: 465-500 inclusive and documents for the years 1040-1073 AD inclusive.

7. McLynn, F. (1998) – *1066 The Year of the Three Battles*, p. 108, Jonathon Cape, London, UK.

8. McLynn, F. op.cit. p.15.

9. Oleson, T.J. (1955) – *The Witanagemot in the Reign of Edward the Confessor*, English Historical Review (EHR), London, UK. Also Bradbury, J. op.cit. p.9, Also McLynn, F. op.cit. p.79.

10. Gillingham, J. (1998) – *The Normans* in "The Lives of the Kings and Queens of England," Fraser, A. (ed.), Weidenfeld & Nicholson Ltd., London, UK.

11.Bradbury, J. op.cit. p.37; also McLynn op. cit. p. 157; also Olsen, T.J. (1953) – *Edward the Confessor's Promise of the throne to Duke William of Normandy*, EHR, 68, pp. 526-545; See also *The Bayeaux Tapestry*.

12.Bradbury, J. *op.cit.* pp. 69-71; also *The Bayeaux Tapestry* for Bayeaux; William of Poitiers in his *Gesta Guillelmi Ducis Normannorum et Regis Anglorum* (1074-1077) says the oath took place at Bonneville-sur-Touques.

13. Bradbury, J. *op. cit.* p.24; see also fig. 1.

14. William of Jumieges (c. 1130) – *Gesta Normannorum Ducum.*

15. McLynn, F. *op. cit.* p. 15; see also *Saxo Grammaticus* (1980) edition Christiansen p. 210.

16. Swanton, M. (2000) – *Anglo-Saxon Chronicle*, New Edition p. 172, Phoenix Press, London, UK; also McLynn, F. op.cit. p. 68.

17. Research by Budapest Campus of the University of Applied Sciences, Belgrade, Yugoslavia (2000) at the request of the author.

Chapter III

"Cur mundus militat sub vana gloria
Cujus prosperitas est transitoria?
Tam cito labitur ejus potentia
Quam vasa figuli quae sunt fragilia."

(From *Puck of Pook's Hill* by Rudyard Kipling)

William the Conqueror, the Normans and their Families

William of Normandy, who later became known as "William the Conqueror," was born in 1027 in Falaise in Normandy.[1] The son of Robert I, Duke of Normandy and his mistress, Herleve, and known throughout his life by his contemporaries as "William the Bastard," even if it was unwise to use that term in his hearing. Herleve was the daughter of Fulbert, a burgess and household official at the Norman court, with the title "Cubicularius," which is something like the later "Yeoman of the Chamber." Contrary to legend she was not the daughter of a tanner and eventually married Herluin, Vicomte de Conteville, by whom she had two sons – Robert, later Count of Mortain and Odo, later Bishop of Bayeaux. No noble of that period would have married the daughter of a tanner.[2] There are still historians who call Fulbert a tanner but should know better.[3] I had thought this popular myth had been killed off years ago, but I still hear it proclaimed, especially on television.

In fact, it is almost certain that Fulbert and Herleve were Jews (see page 36), although this fact may have had to be kept secret and Herleve had probably been baptised.

Robert I, known either as the "Magnificent" or as the "Devil," dependent upon the point of view of the speaker, had almost certainly poisoned his elder brother, Richard III, in order to gain the Dukedom. His father's second wife had been Estrith, the sister of Cnut, and daughter of Sweyn Forkbeard, which gave his father a claim to both Denmark and England.[4] Robert ruled for some 9 years, during which time Normandy descended into almost total anarchy, and to an extent was only saved by the intervention of the Duke's

29

uncle, another Robert, Archbishop of Rouen, who managed to broker a deal not only with Normandy's main neighbour and opponent, Alan of Brittany, but also with some of Robert's most powerful and difficult Barons. Indeed it has always been a suspicion on my part, that it was the Archbishop who persuaded the Duke to go on a pilgrimage to the Holy Land, leaving his young and only son, William, to the protection of the Archbishop of Rouen and Alan of Brittany. The generally accepted idea that the Archbishop and Alan had tried to persuade Robert to stay and govern his Dukedom, but that he had firmly set his mind on a pilgrimage, has always seemed to me to smack of an early form of spin-doctoring. It seems more likely to me that the Archbishop required him to go on a pilgrimage to "atone for his sins." In 1035 therefore, the Duke leaves for the Holy Land and certainly reached both Jerusalem and later Byzantium, where he appears to have met the Emperor Michael IV, but died at Bithynia on his way home. William was now aged 7 and Duke, if he could survive the attempts on his life, and if the Duchy survived.

The History of Normandy is to a very large extent the history of the Viking, as as I outlined in Chapter 1 and, in particular, that of the great Ulvungar dynasty (see Genealogy of the Ulvungars). Perhaps at this point it is as well to look at their origins and the position in Europe at the time our story opens. By 500 AD the Western Roman Empire had to all intents and purposes ceased to exist and it was now a question of who would fill the vacuum.

In the 8th, 9th and early 10th Centuries, what had been the Western Empire had seen a series of onslaughts. The Moslems had attacked from the south and were only turned back by Charles Martel's victory at Poitiers in 732. This victory allowed the formation of the Holy Roman Empire in 800 under Charlemagne, but still the Moslems maintained their hold on the Middle East, North Africa and the Iberian Peninsula and, in the years after 827, they overran Sicily with Palermo falling in 831. It was not until 905 that the reconquest of the Iberian Peninsula started under King Alfonso III of Leon and the Asturias. It would be another 200 years before the Normans conquered Sicily nominally for Christendom, but their Kingdom of Sicily combined Christianity, Islam and Judaism.

The Magyars had come from the East and had attacked and devastated Germany and indeed much of France, until 955 when they were defeated by Otto I, finally settling in Hungary and the surrounding areas. The Serbs had already separated from the Avars and had settled in Bosnia and the surrounding areas.

The Vikings, led by the descendants of the legendary God-King Uôuin of Mesopotamia (Odin or Woden), having established themselves in Scandinavia and the Northern Isles, had come from the North and from 787[5] had attacked most of Europe and by the 9th Century had overrun all of northern Europe from Russia,[6] to Iceland where they first landed in 860, to France and

Britain, which they had been attacking and settling since 787. In 865 Russian Norsemen even attacked and sacked Constantinople. The Vikings had not only just attacked and gone away again, but also had established settlements and trading posts throughout the European coastline and further inland, wherever there were navigable rivers. Their main areas of permanent settlement were Russia, the Orkneys, Caithness and later northern France and Britain, an early Northern Commonwealth (see Chapter VII). For example, the Viking invasion of Britain in 892 consisted not just of warriors but also wives and children in a clear attempt to settle. In 981 they started the Greenland colony. By the beginning of the 10th Century they had re-established the Kingdoms of Mercia and Northumbria, as Jarldoms (Aeldorman or Earl) in England and indeed as we have seen, had become Kings of England as well as their Danish, Norwegian, Swedish and Icelandic possessions, and in France they had been granted land and titles by the last of the Carolignian rulers.

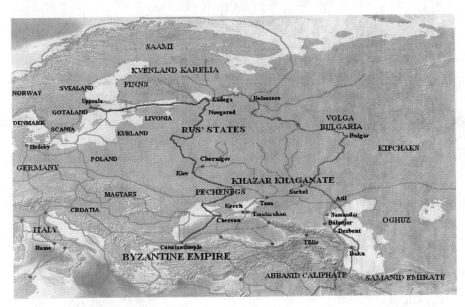

Fig. 5 - The Route from Scandinavia to Constantinople

Rollo was descended from the great Norse family of Ulvungar. He, together with the families of the Beaumont and Montgomery, descended from Herioldus Brocus (see Genealogy Appendix 3) and at various times the members of this dynasty had been Kings or overlords of Russia, Dublin, Denmark, Norway, Sweden, the Isles, Northumbria, Mercia, and East Anglia and effectively controlled a greater area than the Western Roman Empire under the Carolignians.

Rollo (or Hrolf the Red Ganger) was granted land in or about the lower Seine and the city of Rouen, probably with the title Count of Rouen, by Charles the Simple, King of the West Franks, in 911 at the so-called treaty of St. Clair-sur-Epte. But as I pointed out in Chapter 1, Rollo was only one of a number of Norse raiders, who were given grants of land and a title between the period of 850-911. For example, the ancestor of Roger de Montgomery, another Roger (who died in 912), was made Count of Exmes in about 893, before Rollo became Count of Rouen,[7] although Rollo is referred to in Latin documents as Dux Normannorum (Duke or leader of the Normans). Two further grants were made to Rollo's descendants in 924 and 933 by Rudolf, who followed Charles, but the general theory that these grants were made under the terms of the Carolignian system and *pagi*, and that the new rulers were endowed with the powers of the Carolignian counts, has now been questioned and it seems more likely, as I have said previously, that Normandy was formed by an aggressive policy on the part of Rollo's and Roger's descendants.[8] (The whole question as to Rollo's names and the date of his first settlement are dealt with in detail in Notes on Genealogies in the Appendices.)

With the expansion of the Counts of Rouen into the rest of Normandy, first under William Longsword and then under the fifty year reign of Richard, the first Count of Normandy, the Montgomerys become Vicomtes (Vice-Comes) of Hiesmes as well as Counts of Exmes. The Montgomerys and the House of Normandy were already related, as were the Beaumonts (see Genealogies), but the family links between them were strengthened still further when Hugh de Montgomery married Senfrie at the same time as Richard I of Normandy married her younger sister Gunnora, and Turolf de Pont Audemar married the youngest sister Weva. It also gave them, together with the Beaumonts, a somewhat nebulous claim to the thrones of England and Denmark.[9]

The Vicomtes of the regions were responsible directly to the Norman Counts and later the Dukes for the administration of their regions. When the Montgomerys became Vicomte of Hiesmes, the Beaumonts took over their old task as castellans of Exmes, the capital of the Hiesmes region.

It is a very moot point as to the intention of the French Kings when they made these grants of land, but the general consensus is that they were intended to stop further pillages by Norsemen from Scandinavia, by giving those interested some land to call their own in return for protecting France's northern coast against their own kind. However, by 980 or thereabouts the Normans had seized and were holding large tracts of what had been French land and were prepared to defend it, not just against their own kind, but against the French King if need be. I believe that this resolve was strengthened by the death in May of 987 of Louis V, the last of the Carolignians descendents of another Davidic line (see *The God- Kings of Europe*) and the quite illegal declaration by the Archbishop of Rhiems, that the throne of France was elective and not hereditary and the imposition of his candidate Hugh Capet as the new King.[9a] Those in the Church were worried about the resurgence of the "Family." The Normans had also become, at least on the surface, by and large "Good sons of the Church" or at least pretended that they were; for example, they did not generally any longer indulge in polygamy and were marrying into the local aristocracy and accepting their manners and culture. It is however true to say that they felt different to the French around them and never quite accepted the Carolingian ideas and system and the last of the Carolingian Kings were in no position to enforce it.[10] It is also a moot point as to whether the titles "Count of Rouen" and "Count of Exmes" had the same inference of the Carolignian Counts. I think it likely that it was not until Rollo's descendants became and were able to enforce their rights as Counts of Normandy and the Montgomerys accepted the position and title of Vicomtes of Hiesmes that Normandy really started to take shape.

William, now 7, the age at which nobles' children were sent as pages to other nobles' households,[11] could not, as a matter of protection, amongst other things, be sent to another noble's court, as the only suitable court for him would have been that of the French King, and it is doubtful if he would have survived there. It was therefore decided by his guardians that three young cousins should be brought up and educated together with William by a monk called Ralph Moine, who was proud to say that he taught them to read and write in both Latin and Norman-French.[12] These were William FitzOsbern, Roger de Montgomery, and the slightly older Roger de Beaumont. These four were to become William's closest companions and confidants and the only people whom William fully trusted.

It is interesting that William's father, Duke Robert, did not take his most trusted friends with him on his pilgrimage, but rather left them to protect his son and which rather lends support to my theory regarding this pilgrimage. The principal guardians were, apart from the Archbishop and Alan of Brittany, Osbern Herfasston the Steward, Gilbert de Brionne, Turold of Neuf-marche, Ralph Tesson, Hugh Bishop of Avranches, Richard of St. Valery-en-Caux, Roger Vetulus , Viscounts Neil, Gozelin and Thurstin, and Edward, later King of England. Robert also obtained the agreement of Henry I, King of France to the effect that William would be his successor and in 1036, William attended the French court to take his vow of fealty as the next Duke.

William survived thanks to his guardians, who not only managed his Duchy for him but kept any rebellion in check and indeed managed to enforce the Ducal rights in Lower Normandy and bring it under control in William's last year as a minor. Though according to William of Jumieges, three of his guardians paid for this loyalty with their lives (Gilbert de Brionne, Turold and his steward Osbern).

The most important victory in William's early reign was probably that of Val-es-Dunes in 1047, when William's suzerain, King Henry I of France, came to his young vassal's aid. One has to wonder whether Henry regretted this at a later date, when he joined the enemies of William in 1052 and 1053.

William's uncle, another William, this time of Arques, had never accepted the succession of his brother's illegitimate, minor son and this opposition turned to rebellion. (This suggests that Papaia was a second wife and not a concubine as otherwise, William of Arques would himself have been illegitimate.) In 1053, Henry I tried unsuccessfully to relieve the Castle of Arques, but was decisively beaten by William at the battle of St.-Aubin-sur-Scie. In this battle William used the tactics of the feigned flight, which was to become so important 13 years later. Although not the end of William's troubles, the surrender of Arques and the submission of Count William was a turning point in opposition to William. The next year saw William not only victorious again, but to an extent, sent real fears into his enemies. At the battle of Mortemer the invading army was, according to William of Poitiers, decimated. At midnight William had a herald proclaim the details of the victory from the top of a tree whereupon the defeated king fled the field.[13]

One of the most important prisoners captured during this battle was Count Guy de Ponthieu, a descendent of Charlemagne, who submitted to William and became his vassal. Count Guy's daughter Agnes would later marry Robert de Montgomery, eldest son of Roger de Montgomery (and usually known as Robert de Bellême).[14] Importantly it was on his territory that Harold Godwinsson was shipwrecked and William was able, as a result of this submission, to demand that Harold be handed over to him. Harold was treated extremely well by William, who personally knighted him and took him on campaign with him. Whether William wanted to see how Harold behaved on campaign or whether this was simply to establish a friendship with a powerful Anglo-Saxon noble who might help him some time in the future is unclear; indeed, it may simply have been that Harold was an Ulvungar cousin. All that can be stated with certainty is that William assessed Harold's military abilities, knighted him and obtained Harold's oath that he would support William's claim to the English throne.

Bayeaux Tapestry Photo 2
Harold in Pontieu

By 1066 therefore, William, now 39, was at the height of his powers. By a series of victories and marriages he had established his rule firmly in Normandy and had seen off the threats from France, Anjou and Brittany. He had married Matilda of Flanders, apparently a love match and which gave him access to Flanders' sea power and trade.

His cousin Roger de Montgomery had married Mabile of Bellême, another love match, bringing the powerful Talvais family into the Norman family fold. His other cousins had also married into powerful families whose support would be necessary should William need to invade England.

It is worthwhile looking a little more closely at some of these marriages. Whether William had agreed a match with Matilda's father beforehand has always been a matter for speculation, but apparently when William's proposal was made to her, Matilda turned him down on account of his bastardy. William took umbrage at this and rode to Matilda's father's castle, broke in upon her, proceeded to whip her with his leather crop and then leave. This treatment apparently endeared him to Matilda so much that she promptly fell in love with him and agreed to marry him and – although so small that she would be considered a dwarf by today's standards – gave him four sons and six daughters. The above story may be apocryphal but shows something about William's temper and will.

Roger de Montgomery's wooing is, however, a matter of historical fact. The powerful Talvais family of Bellême, descended from Yves de Bellême, Governor of Creil and Grandmaster of crossbowmen, who had married Godehilde, descended from the Merovignian, Chlothar IV[15] owned not only the great fortress at Bellême but also Alençon and Domfront. As was not unusual in France of the time, the Talvais owed fealty to the King for Bellême, to the Count of Maine for Domfront and to the Duke of Normandy for Alençon.

In 1051 William was busy fighting Geoffrey Martel and laid siege to Domfront, which both the Bellêmes and Geoffrey Martel of Maine believed impregnable. William settled down for a long siege, then typically left Roger de Montgomery in charge of the siege and made a lightning dash to Alençon, catching the town unawares and almost managing to gallop his cavalry into the town. In fact possibly some of his soldiers did manage to get in unbeknownst to the townspeople who, stupidly thinking that William could not besiege two places at once taunted William about his bastardy, hanging out hides over the walls and shouting "Hides! Hides for the Tanner!" (It is from this event that later historians derive the idea that William's mother was the daughter of a tanner. However, as I showed in *The God Kings of Europe*, what they were really saying was that William's mother was Jewish because the job of tanner was almost exclusively done by Jews at the time. Effectively, they were saying, "Jew Boy, come and get us!") At all events, much to the horror of the townspeople, the gates were opened from the inside, either by William's soldiers or possibly a group of Tanners, and William took the town.

In revenge for the insult to his mother, he had thirty-two of the leading citizens paraded in front of the townspeople and had their hands and feet cut off. William then threatened the garrison with the same fate if they did not surrender immediately. Not surprisingly the garrison surrendered and then sent a delegation to Domfront at William's orders, warning the garrison there, that they too would suffer that fate unless they surrendered as well. The men of Domfront asked for guarantees, which William gave them in return for Roger de Montgomery getting Mabile de Talvaise as his bride and with her the castles of Alençon and Bellême.

The same sort of alliances were being forged by the Beaumonts and the FitzOsborns (William Fitz Osborn had married Aeliz, daughter of Roger de Tosny) and William's half-brother, Count of Mortain (or Mortagne) had married Maud de Montgomery. One could say that William's social, political and military structure was totally "Family" orientated, with all those in positions of power connected to him by blood. This was a typical Davidic/ Ulvunger strategy, but woe betide those who broke their oaths of loyalty. They were dealt with swiftly and ruthlessly by sword, rope or poison. The Norman Families, like many modern families, frequently feuded, but the difference between them and the modern family was that there was little to stop these feuds from becoming bloody in the extreme.

During William's minority Gilbert of Brionne and Fulk, the 3rd son of Giroie, were both killed by Odo the Fat and Robert, the 4th son of Giroie. What is more, this killing was planned by Rudolf de Gace, 2nd son of the Archbishop of Rouen, yet both Robert of Rouen and Gilbert de Brionne were guardians of the young Duke William.

At Val-es-Dunes, William's cousin of Burgundy, who thought that he should be Duke, was the principle rebel aided by Hamon-aux-Dents and his brother, also William's cousins. Interestingly, the battle of Val-es-Dunes was not really won by King Henry on behalf of his young vassal, but by Ralph

Tesson, switching sides halfway through the battle and attacking Burgundy's supporters from the rear. Did Duke William engineer this switch, one wonders? It is not beyond the bounds of possibilities, after all, Ralph was supposed to be one of the Duke's guardians. Certainly Ralph obtained his reward by being given as his bride the daughter of William's maternal uncle, thus bringing him firmly into the family.

Another of these feuds was between the de Tosnys and Grandmesnils on the one side, and the Beaumonts on the other. Roger de Tosny had earlier (1040-41) rebelled against William on account of William's bastardy. The rebellion was quickly squashed by the Beaumonts, but something had to be done. The obvious solution was to form some dynastic marriages, so Hugh de Grandmesnil marries Adelise de Beaumont and just to be on the safe side, William FitzOsbern, William's trusted friend and cousin, marries Aeliz de Tosny. Ralf de Tosny's daughter, Godvere, meanwhile, is married to another cousin, this time the son of Eustace of Boulogne, Baldwin. Although these dynastic marriages did not always work, they played an important part in securing the co-operation of these Norman magnates. There was, however, nothing new in this. The Scandinavians and Davidic families had been doing this for generations (see Genealogies at the end).

It has always struck me as amazing the way that William managed to keep Roger de Montgomery and William FitzOsbern from feuding. William de Montgomery, Roger's uncle, had assassinated William FitzOsbern's father in the Duke's own bedchamber and FitzOsbern's provost had in turn killed William de Montgomery and his group of friends. Apparently, William and Roger decided that honour had been satisfied and as they were both being brought up with William in the FitzOsbern household, decided they would be better off burying the hatchet.

I have mentioned the various brides of these magnates, but what sort of women were they? Mere pawns in the marriage game, or were they players? I believe that they were much more than pawns. In my book *The God Kings of Europe*, I postulated a sacred triangle and a female descent, which carried on the knowledge of their Jewish Davidic inheritance. If we go back a couple of generations and look at Emma of Normandy, we shall have a very fair idea of the way in which many of these strong minded women operated.

Emma had been extremely young when she went as a bride to Aethelred II. For her this was a major triumph. To become Queen of one of the wealthiest realms in Europe was the dream of any young girl. She was also fulfilling the dynastic requirements of the House of Normandy by an alliance with the Anglo-Saxon ruling house, which after all, was in contention with the Scandinavian Ulvungars, her own family.

When Aethelred fled to Normandy, I do not suppose she was very impressed and was only too happy to become the wife of his successor, Cnut. Did she know that Cnut was already married to Aelgifa of Northampton? I am sure that she did. But Aelgifa was to be left in Denmark as Regent, and Emma could now resume her place as Queen of England. The church even married them knowing that Cnut was already married. No doubt they were happy to pretend that, because they had not married Aelgifa and Cnut. That marriage was non-existent, or perhaps Cnut simply said "Marry us or I'll cut your head off." It's amazing how quickly you can persuade people who are threatened with their life! The apex of the sacred triangle had been formed.

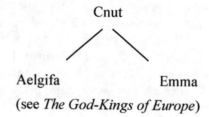

Cnut

Aelgifa   Emma

(see *The God-Kings of Europe*)

Emma was evidently a woman to take up cudgels either on her own behalf or that of her family. When Harold Harefoot took over the throne of England from her own son Harthacnut, she persuaded the Normans to launch an attack on England together with her sons by Aethelred. This attack was, unfortunately for Emma, half-hearted both by the Normans and her own son Edward, who, as soon as the going got tough, fled back to Normandy. It was only when her son by Cnut, Harthacnut, arrived in England with a large following, that she was able to regain her position as Queen Mother.

Harthacnut re-established her in a position of power, even having his brother's body dug up and thrown into a bog, no doubt egged on by Emma. Unfortunately, when her son Edward came to the throne he did not much appreciate her interference, particularly as she backed Magnus for the throne against him. Maybe she thought she could persuade Magnus to marry her and make her Queen for the 3rd time. She evidently preferred her men strong. It would appear that she also took a number of lovers after Cnut's death, thereby forming the bottom half of the sacred triangle. Edward, by all accounts, did not much care for women. He stripped her of all her wealth and had her confined to a nunnery.

Then there was Poppa, the 1st wife or, again, possibly mistress of Rollo I (see Genealogy I). There is little known about Poppa. You cannot even find her as a separate entry in the Encyclopaedia Britannica. According to the little information that is available, she was the daughter of Berenger of Bayeaux. Even this is not very helpful, as we know nothing about Berenger. Poppa was apparently red haired and petite and was initially a captive of Rollo on one of his raids. He apparently fell in love with her and certainly she was the only one to give him children.

Again, I suspect that Rollo went through some sort of Scandinavian marriage ceremony with her, for there seems to be not the slightest hint of problems with their son, William Longsword, being illegitimate. Rollo was known as Hrolf the Ganger because he was so large that he could not find a horse big enough for him (Ganger means Horse – so he was his own horse), so we have this giant of a man apparently in love with a small bird of a woman. Yet this woman, about whom we know so little, was the mother of the House of Normandy. Without her there would have been no Normandy, no Dukedom and no conquest of England.

Another very important woman in the families was of course William the Conqueror's wife, Matilda. About her we know quite a lot. She was the daughter of Count Baldwin of Flanders and niece of the French King, Henry. She was brought up in her father's court in Flanders and apparently could read and write in both French and Latin, as well as Flemish. She had spent some time in the French court and was somewhat vain in her dress.

She was also by our standards, a dwarf, being only four foot two inches high. William by contrast was five foot eleven inches tall. It seems that like his ancestor Rollo, he liked his ladies petite. William apparently saw her at a gathering in her father's palace and fell in love with her and asked her father for her hand. Baldwin, who desperately needed allies at the time and saw in William a strong ally and warrior, was only too happy to agree.

Unfortunately, Matilda was not so immediately smitten and told her father that she was the daughter of a ruling count with the blood of Charlemagne in her veins and niece of the King and was not going to marry some bye-blow of an upstart Duke. The result, when reported to William, caused the scene that I have related earlier. There is some disagreement as to whether Matilda fell for him before their wedding or whether she came to love him after that. Certainly there was real affection between them and she was one of the few people that William trusted, making her Regent of Normandy during his absences in England.

In fact, so far as I am aware she only set foot in England once, in 1068, when she was crowned at Westminster Abbey, when the English were amazed that this tiny woman was their Queen and wife of the powerful King William. Small she may have been, but she bore William four sons and six daughters. Having been brought up in the Court at Flanders, she was well aware of how things were managed in the Charlemagnic tradition and brought a certain graciousness to what would otherwise have been a court of fairly rude warriors. She was also very friendly with another important lady at William's court, Mabile de Montgomery, the wife of Roger de Montgomery.

Much has been written about Mabile, most of it bad, though I suspect that a great deal of the bad press came from Ebrard de Montgomery, son of Roger by his second wife, Adeliza de Puiset. Ebrard was intensely jealous of his eldest half-brother Robert of Bellême and for some reason hated Robert's mother, Mabile. It is Ebrard who called Mabile the "Daughter of Satan." Ebrard was a priest and chaplain to both William II and Henry I and supported them against his own family and particularly against his half-brother Robert. Brainwashed by the Church I suppose!

Mabile was the daughter of Guilluime II de Talvas (or Talvais), the Prince of Bellême (1033-1053) by his second wife, the daughter of Raoul de Beaumont, and so already had Ulvungar blood in the Family. The Talvas were not Normans in the sense that they were of Scandinavian origin. Their line descends from Yves de Bellême (d.940) who was Governor of Creil, and Grand Master of Crossbowmen. In fact, the great keep at Bellême, defended by these famous crossbowmen, was almost impregnable. Yves had married Godehilde, the four times great-grand-daughter of the Merovignian, Chlothar IV, hence the title Prince, and their son, Guilluime I, had been made Seigneur of Bellême and Alençon by Robert the Pious (see Belleme Genealogy).

Roger de Montgomery apparently became attracted to her when she attended a court function at William's court and demanded of William her hand in marriage. The story of their wooing I have already recounted, but it would appear that once she became Roger's wife, she threw herself life and soul into promoting the Montgomery cause including, according to some authorities, not being above administering a little poison, when it seemed to be required. One must however be careful about these accusations of poison. If you read the stories carefully, some at least read more like food poisoning. With little or no hygiene in the 11th Century, I can only say that I am surprised that more people didn't die from it.

She was also not afraid of putting herself in the front line. When Roger was away in England she not only acted as his Regent, but when Montgomery lands were attacked, herself donned mail and led the Montgomery troops into battle. Unfortunately, this also led to her downfall and she was killed at the Chateau de Bures-sur-Dives in 1082.

One of the interesting things about the Talvas is that although they were not pagan in the way that the Scandinavian ancestors of the Normans were pagans, worshipping Odin and Thor, they were members of a non-Roman church. It is not clear whether they were Jewish or Cathars or, what seems most likely, according to the latest research, members of a Judaic-Christian sect called the Elchasaites, after the followers of Elchasai, the mentor of Mani.[15] I suspect that to Ebrard, a pious clerk, this was not just heresy, but the dark workings of Satan, hence his calling her "Daughter of Satan."

William's mother too, was by all accounts a strong character. She was the daughter of Fulbert, a burgess and household official at the Norman Court whose title "Cubicularius" was something like Yeoman of the Chamber, or perhaps even Chamberlain. There are those who ask that if this was so, then why did Robert not marry her – but I think this is looking with modern eyes at the question. If Robert was married or, at the very least, handfasted to Estrith, the half-sister of Cnut, then there was no way in which he could get rid of Estrith without causing enormous offence to both the Danish and English Royal Families, the senior Ulvungar lines, and the Church, by now, would not accept polygamy. If she was a Jewess, as I have indicated, it is probable that the Church would have been against so powerful a union. This being so, he had to get rid of Herleve. I believe that he agreed to her marrying one of his staunchest, but not very powerful vassals, Herluin, Vicomte de Conteville, in return for considerable advancement and agreed that their sons would be advanced as if they were his own. I believe also that this was one of the reasons for him agreeing to go on a pilgrimage. In the event it was left to his illegitimate son, William was to advance his legitimate half-brothers.

Until Robert decided to make William his heir, shortly before leaving for Jerusalem, William had lived mostly with his mother and her family. After this, he was to spend most of his young life under the roof of the Osberns. That Herleve was held in high esteem, as were her brothers, is attested to by the fact that her brothers actually acted as attesters to a charter of the infant William and she herself was made a guardian for Matilda by the Count of Flanders. This was very much the sort of thing done by a modern Chamberlain. Her two sons by Herluin became Counts and Earls in their own right, one of them Robert, Count of Mortain, marrying back into the Ulvungar Family by marrying Maud de Montgomery, one of Roger de Montgomery's daughters. According to some researchers, Herleve married again on the death of Herluin.

Duke William also had a full sister, Adele, who had married Enguerrand, the son of Count Hugh of Pontieu and his wife, Berta of Aumale. They had one daughter, Ada.

When Enguerrand was ambushed and killed in 1053, Adele married Lambert of Lens, younger brother of Count Eustace II of Boulogne. Lambert was killed in his turn in 1054, but not before he managed to father another daughter, Judith. After his death, Adele, still very young, married for a third time – this time to Odo of Champagne, by whom she had a son, Stephen.[17] William, therefore, had been concerned to keep Pontieu under his control. First, by marrying Adele to Enguerrand and then, by marrying Robert de Bellême to Agnes. He also later, after the conquest, had to try to keep the remaining Anglo-Saxons happy and bestowed the hand of his beloved niece, Judith, on the one person who, via both Danish and Anglo-Saxon descent, could legitimately claim the throne – namely, Waltheof, Earl of Huntingdon.

Waltheof was by all accounts handsome, but it would seem not to Judith's liking after the marriage – indeed, according to some, Judith hated him. They had three daughters, Maud, born in 1074, Alice in 1075 and Judith, about 12 to 18 months later. Judith lived up to her Norman ancestry and when her chance came she took it.

Waltheof attended or possibly hosted a wedding feast for Emma, the daughter of William FitzOsbern and Ralf de Gael. The wedding, at Exning in Cambridgeshire, apparently was against the Duke's wishes. Not only that, but at the meeting a plan was hatched by Ralf de Gael and Roger of Hereford, the brother of the bride and son of William FitzOsbern and Waltheof, to overthrow William and restore an Anglo-Saxon (Waltheof?) to the throne. Waltheof apparently lost his courage and blabbed the whole story to William. The rebellion was crushed. Ralf escaped with his bride and went on crusade, dying in the Holy Land. Roger FitzOsbern was blinded and spent the rest of his life in prison (note, once again, the blinding). Waltheof would have escaped scot-free and been given rewards by William were it not for Judith. She accused her own husband in front of the Witanagemot. They declined to find Waltheof guilty, so she then accused him in front of the Norman Barons. They found him guilty in 1076 and condemned him to death. The execution followed quickly and Waltheof was beheaded on the last day of May. Judith had had her revenge.[18]

Roger de Montgomery had both brothers and a sister. The latter, whose name was, it is thought, Matilda, was married to Charles le Ufroy, who together with Roger and his son, Robert of Bellême, designed and were responsible for building the great castle at Gisors (see Genealogy – Montgomery, Counts of Bellême). Gisors was, in fact, an updated version of Bellême and the vision of Gisors can be seen clearly by studying the remains of the two castles concerned.

This then was the "Family" which prepared for their greatest test in January of 1066.

References: Chapter 3

1. McLynn, F. *op. cit.* p. 21, but Maurice Ashley says 1028, see Ashley, M. (1973) – *The Life and Times of William I*, p. 52, Weidenfeld & Nicholson, London, UK.

2. See also McLynn, F. *op. cit.* p. 23.

3. Ashley, M. *op.cit.* p. 52.

4. Cannon, J., & Griffiths, R. (1988) – *The Oxford Illustrated History of the British Monarchy*, p. "Genealogies," Oxford University Press, Oxford, UK.

5. Castleden, R. (1994), *World History*, A chronological Dictionary of dates, Parragon, London, UK.

6. In 850, Rurik (a Norseman) takes over from Keitel (Ascold) as ruler of Kiev and later founds the city of Novgorod in 862, becoming "Grand Prince" and starting what is to become the Russian Royal Family. See also Castleden, R. op. cit.

7. Montgomery, H. (2002) – *The Montgomery Millennium*, p.v, Megatrend, Belgrade & London.

8. Allen Brown, R. (1984) – *The Normans*, p. 17, Boydell Press, Suffolk, UK; see also Le Patourel, J. (1983) – *Norman Empire*, Chapter 1.

9. Montgomery, H. *op. cit.* p. 1. See also Records at College of Arms, London. Also see notes on Genealogy.

9.a New research which will come out in a future book suggests that there may have been other reasons for the Archbishop's decision.

10. McLynn, F. *op. cit.* p. 27; also McKitterick, R. (1983) – *The Frankish Kingdoms under the Carolingians* 751–987, Longman Group UK Ltd., Essex, UK; also Loud, G.A. (1981) – *Gens Normannorum*, Anglo-Saxon Studies 4, pp. 104 – 116.

11. Duane, O.B. (1997) – *Chivalry* p. 45, Brockhampton Press, London, UK.

12. McLynn, F. *op. cit.* p. 30.

13. William of Poitiers, *op. cit.* pp. 73-75.

14. Montgomery, H. *op. cit.* p. 3; Agnes was the sole heir of Guy and as William's vassal, her marriage was in William's grant. Her marriage to the eldest son of one of his main supporters cemented his grip on Ponthieu. The son of Agnes and Robert, called William, of course, married the daughter of Eudo I, Duke of Burgundy.

15. *Chahiers Percherons* (1976) – Triem. No. 51, 3eme. Trimestre, 1976, Assoc. de Amis du Perche. Library of the Marie de Belleme.

16. Stoyanov, Y. (1994) – *The Hidden Tradition in Europe*, pp. 87-88, Penguin, London, UK.

17. Platts, B. (1985) – *Scottish Hazard*, Vol. 1, pp. 38, Procter Press, London, UK.

18. Platts, B. ibid. Chap. 3. See also Ashley, M. (1972) – *The Life and Times of William I*, p. 92, Weidenfeld & Nicholson, London, UK.

Chapter IV

I followed my Duke ere I was a lover,
To take from England fief and fee;

(From Sir Richard's song – *Puck of Pook's Hill* by Rudyard Kipling)

Preparation for the Invasion by William and the Normans

William, as soon as he heard of Edward's death, sent a message to both Harold and Edward's Norman Barons claiming the throne and reminding Harold of his oath.

Harold, by the time he received this message, had already been proclaimed King, as Harold II, and therefore rejected William's claim. William now prepared to invade and sets his date for August.

There were, however, two others who also decided to claim the throne. Harold Hardrada, King of Norway, took up Magnus's claim and Sweyn Estrithsson, King of Denmark (see Chapter 1). Harold Hardrada did not initially take up Magnus's claim until persuaded by Tostig, the brother of "King" Harold, for reasons of his own.[1] It is my opinion that William either sent Tostig to Harald to ask for Harald's help with a pincer movement invasion from both North and South to divide Harold Godwinsson's forces and was prepared to divide England, or had in mind some sort of sharing arrangement. Harald was, after all, married to an Ulvungar.

Sweyn Estrithsson, who had suffered a severe defeat at the hands of Harold Hardrada, was not really in a position to do more than posture and was more than happy to accept William's overtures on the basis that if William was successful then he, Sweyn, will give up his claim to William, presumably for some pecuniary benefit. But it should be mentioned that he did attempt an invasion later on.

Harold Hardrada, on the other hand, had to be taken very seriously. He raised an army and fitted out the necessary ships to invade England. The difference between the methods of preparation of the two invaders could not be greater.

William's preparation was more akin to a modern General, with a General Staff, an inner circle and with allied troops controlled by his men or, at the very least, with liaison men to see that his orders were carried out.

William's Staff and Inner Circle consisted entirely of Family: Robert de Beaumont who was to remain behind as Head of the Regency Council to assist the Duchess, Matilda, together with Hugh d'Avranches. Robert d'Eu was in charge of the advanced camp at Saint-Valery. William FitzOsbern was in charge of Logistics once they reached England. Roger de Montgomery was in charge of Logistics and Strategy at the assembly point in Dives.

It is also worthwhile looking at the logistics that William and his "General Staff" had to overcome. William had to bring together a large Army of diverse backgrounds – not only Norman but also Breton, Flemish, Boulagnaise and assorted French and other mercenaries from all over Europe. They had to be assembled at Dives and provided with tents, wine or beer, bread and meat, etc. Metal smiths and armourers had to be on hand to shoe horses and mend or make the chain mail, helmets and to repair swords and lances. Bowmakers and fletchers had to be provided as well as barber surgeons.

The Bayeaux Tapestry shows men cutting down trees and making boats, which were to be assembled at Dives and then only moved to St. Valery prior to embarkation (see Map 1). The reasons for choosing Dives were several. Firstly, it gave on to the Caen hinterland from which would come the corn, meat, etc. needed to support the troops. Secondly, it had a harbour with a natural barrier which protected it and ships moored there from not only storms, but from prying eyes and thirdly, it made attack on the ships from the seaward side very difficult. (Regretfully, this harbour barrier no longer exists.) William expected Harold to have spies in his camp and possibly to mount an attack on his, William's, ships before they could put to sea.

How many men, horses and ships did William have? I'm afraid we don't actually know and figures vary widely from as little as 5,000 to a many as 50,000 men, but I believe that the most likely number was somewhere between 10,000 to 17,000 and were probably divided as follows:

3,000-4,000 mounted men (Knights, men-at-arms and Serjeants), 6,000-8,000 foot soldiers, about 1,000-2,000 archers and cross-bowmen, and anywhere from 1,000-3,000 support staff.[2]

It is worthwhile looking at what these figures mean in terms of logistics and what was achieved. Let us take the number of 3,000 horses for a start. If you are going on an expedition such as this and are going to depend on your Destrier in battle, you would want him shoed before embarkation. In those days they used 15 oz. horseshoes and each of those had 6 nails to hold them on. The horseshoes themselves, plus the nails to hold them on, all had to be hand made: (6 x 4 x 3000 = 72,000 nails) + (4 x 3000 = 12,000 horseshoes) – some 8 tons of iron.[3]

How many smiths would have to be employed to produce these? I have got no idea, but suspect a great number. I imagine a separate village of blacksmiths each with his furnace, anvil and hammers. I can see the apprentices unbanking the fires early in the morning, getting out the bellows and starting the furnaces going, whilst others would go to the river to fetch water in large wooden pails ready for the iron to be quenched, as the master blacksmith fashioned the horseshoes in rough – or perhaps the greater blacksmiths used journeymen or their own apprentices in the early stages and only themselves actually did the shoeing. The noise, the smoke and the bustle around this village must have been amazing and had probably never been seen before. Prof. McLynn calculated that it would have taken 10 blacksmiths, working a 10 hour day, the whole of August just to shoe the horses, so we have to be looking at double that number, even if some were apprentices.

Then there would be the Horselines. The great Destriers would need cover and constant attention. They would have to be exercised daily. They would have to be fed.

Each Destrier would require 5.5 kilos of grain per day (5.5 x 3,000 = 16,500 kilos of grain *each and every day* they were at Dives). Plus fresh water by the ton.

But horses also get rid of large amounts of waste. Anyone who has looked after horses will know. I believe someone calculated that Roger de Montgomery's staff had to organise the disposal of some 5,000 cartloads of Manure and some 3,182,000 litres of urine.

In the days of proper British Cavalry regiments, one of the questions that all young subalterns had to answer to pass their Captaincy exam was, "How often does a horse defecate per 24 hours and how much manure does it produce?" Now I realise why they used to ask that question!

The real success of this organisation was that there was no disease, except for the odd case of French pox. Compare this to the Crimea 800 years later when more perished from disease than were killed in action.

Imagine, too, the great tented encampments for the troops! There would be on average 10 men per tent so for 10,000 men (the Knights and Barons would have had their own) you would require 1,000-1,500 tents and each tent consisted of 36 hides stitched together (36,000-54,000 hides) and were probably made from the hides of the animals slaughtered for meat. Each group would have been assigned tents according to how they were going to embark, or around the flag of the leader under whom they would serve.

I mentioned earlier the Bayeaux Tapestry showing trees being felled to be turned into ships, and one would like to know how many ships there were. Wace, for example, writing in 1150, quotes the figure of 696 vessels, but most historians disagree with this figure. We do not even know what type of vessels were available to William or what type he could build in the time, but we can make some informed guesses.

Some would have been cargo vessels, which regularly plied the trade between France/Flanders and Britain or as far as Scandinavia. These he would have requisitioned. It is most likely this type of vessel that would have been used to carry the horses and stores and probably the grooms to look after the horses. This type of boat would transport between 5-10 horses plus fodder, saddlery, etc., and the men to look after them, plus probably some archers or men-at-arms as protection. Let us say a maximum of 10 horses, 10 grooms and 10 archers/infantry. So for 3,000 horses you need at least 300 plus boats. However, some of the boats would have been much larger. There is no reason to suppose that the Normans had lost the art of shipbuilding of their Viking ancestors and we know that the average Viking longboat had a fighting crew of 90 (see, for example, the excavation of the Gokstadt ship in Norway). (4) Olaf Tryggvason's ship, "The Long Serpent," had a crew of 300. It is equally likely, however, that many vessels would have been smaller, perhaps taking only 30-50 men. Again, if we average at say, 80, then we need 125 vessels to transport 10,000. Add to this a lower average for the number of horses per vessel and the fact that there may well have been more than 3,000 horses, then perhaps Wace's figure of 696 was not so wrong after all.

In 1061 another Norman force had successfully invaded the Island of Sicily from mainland Italy. The leaders of this expedition were Roger and Robert de Hautville. They were related closely to the Norman Ducal Family and we know that they continued communication with their cousins in Normandy. Their experience, I feel, would have been very useful to William in planning the Invasion of England.

Let us now look at how the force was constituted and who were William's allies and commanders. It must be emphasised that this was not a feudal host, indeed many of William's Barons flatly refused to go abroad, saying that this was not part of their feudal obligation. William FitzOsbern was appointed by the Barons to take their arguments to William, but FitzOsbern persuaded them to agree to his acting with their "de facto" power of attorney, which was foolish, as they knew he was not only William's close cousin, but that he was totally loyal to William. There is some disagreement about what then happened, but at all events the Barons finished up not only agreeing to go with William, but even agreeing to provide twice their quota of men that they would have had to as a purely feudal host.(5) In return they would be granted land and titles in England. It was, in fact, the first venture capital joint stock unlimited company formed for a particular enterprise, namely "The Conquest of England Company Unlimited."

Who else was providing troops? Well, William's father-in-law, the Count of Flanders for one, though he did not himself go over to England with William. Then there was, of course, Eustace of Boulogne, whose own hope of claiming the throne for his family evaporated with the death of Godgifu, without heirs. He took over a large group of Boulognaise and, although given a command by William on the right wing of his host, William took the precaution of appointing Roger de Montgomery as joint commander of the right wing with, I suspect, a brief to keep a watch on Eustace. Roger commanded not only the Knights and men at arms from his own domains, including the contingent of Bellême crossbowmen, but also the contingent of Roger de Beaumont, who had to stay behind as part of the Regency Council. The Beaumont contingent was led by Roger's son, who made a considerable name for himself at Hastings.

There was also Viscount Aimeri de Thouars, from the Aquitaine. Aimeri is interesting for a number of reasons. First, he was almost certainly a descendent of the Nasi or ruler of Septimania under Pepin the Short and Charlemagne. His seal was apparently a Lion Rampant with a star above it (see Appendix 15). Pepin's sister Adela had married the Nasi or Prince of Septimania, and Charlemagne had married a daughter of the Nasi.[6] The Normans and the Aquitainians had intermarried as well, and at the time, he and William were cousins and the Normans had helped their kinsmen fighting against the Saracens on the border there (a continuation of the policy of Peppin and Charlemagne). Thouars was a fortified town commanding the river Thouet and the main routes between Aquitaine and Poitou. Aimeri was a very powerful Lord controlling some 17 castles, hundreds of square miles of territory and scores of noble vassals. He became such an important part of what Professor McLynn calls the "Crusade," that he won his place amongst the "Companions of the Conqueror."[7]

I suspect, also, that many of his Knights would have been descendants of the famed Jewish warriors of Septimania,[8] who would perhaps have seen the conquest of England as a chance to start again in a new land, away from church persecutions and problems. These problems had started to become serious as the powers of the Church increased and the last of the Carolignians descended into chaos. William would be a King who was sympathetic to them. Certainly William invited Jews to come and settle in England and they remained there in one form or another during the period of the Norman Kings. They were even called, by the Norman Kings, "His Jews."[9]

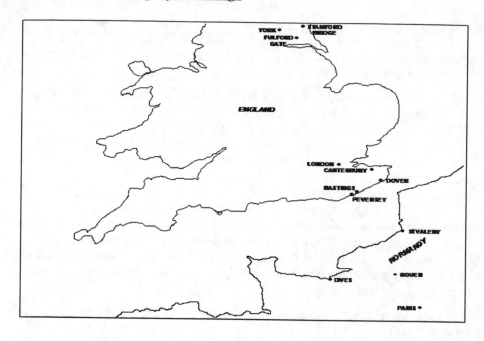

Fig. 6 - Invasion Map

The above were William's allies. Who then, were his commanders in the field?

Apart from William himself, in overall command, and Eustace and Aimeri in charge of their own contingents, there were the following: Robert of Mortain, William's half-brother who married Maud de Montgomery; Hugh de Montfort, one of the great Barons of Normandy; William FitzOsbern, William's cousin, who married Aeliz de Tosny; Ralf de Tosny, whose daughter Godvere was to marry Count Eustace's son, Baldwin, later King of Jerusalem; Hugh de Grandmesnil, married to Adelise de Beaumont; Odo, Bishop of Bayeaux, William's other half-brother; Geoffrey, Bishop of Coutances; Walter Giffard and Roger de Montgomery. Each and every one was related to the other either by blood or by marriage. It is also interesting to note that at least two of the military commanders, Odo and Geoffrey, were churchmen. According to the Church, they must not shed Christian blood and in order to overcome this, the bishops used maces to crack open the heads of their opponents but did not use a sword, thus theoretically not shedding blood directly. The Bayeaux tapestry shows Odo using a mace.

The Army arrived at the mustering point at Dives on the 4th & 5th August and remained there for a month until about 8th-10th of September, when they moved to the advance camp at Saint-Valery (see map).

Historians seem to disagree as to the reason for William's long wait at Dives. One of the main reasons given was that the wind was against him. The problem for modern readers is that we are fed daily with a surfeit of weather charts on television, and we are perfectly well aware that there is a continental weather system that embraces Northern Europe, the British Isles and Scandinavia. We also know that Harold Hardrada had to wait. Now it is simply impossible to imagine that if Harold did not have an offshore wind from North to South, then there must have been an offshore wind from South to North. They cannot both have had unfavourable winds!

What therefore was the real reason? We don't actually know, but I suspect that William was waiting for information. We know that Tostig, his uncle by marriage, was with Harald Hardrada and if I am correct in my surmise that a double invasion was planned, then both Harald and William would have been waiting for confirmation that the other's fleet was ready. Thereafter, it would be up to the winds. Nor do I think that all the vessels were ready much before the beginning of September.

We know that Edward the Confessor had appointed many Normans to positions of power in England. We can readily believe that the Anglo-Saxon King Harold would be busy replacing them and that therefore, they would act as a fifth column or as spies for William. Now I believe that William was aware that (a) Harold had summoned out the Fyrd and that (b) he had his ships patrolling the approaches to the English coast line.

In fact, we know that he had captured some spies of Harold because he let one go deliberately.[10] Furthermore, he had already arranged with Tostig to mount a probing raid on the Isle of Wight in May, with help from Flanders. So Tostig went to Denmark and gained Hadrada's agreement to a joint invasion, then waited to see that Hardrada was getting ready and agreed a probable date. He then, either himself, came back to William, or more likely sent a messenger and mounted his mini-invasion, probing for King Harold's response. King Harold's response was fast and overwhelming and Tostig retired to Scotland to await Harold Hardrada. At least one scholar has suggested that William originally intended also to invade using the Isle of Wight. Perhaps this was so. Perhaps he let Tostig use this method to see if it was feasible, but bluntly, this is speculation.

William had his own spies, we even know the name of one of them, Robert fitz Wimarc,[11] and would know that Harold had to disband the Fyrd (a) because they were required to bring in the harvest but (b) more importantly, Harold's commissariat was not the equal of William's, and by the end of August he had no longer the wherewithal to feed them. The Anglo-Saxon Chronicle says, "The mens provisions were gone, and no one could hold them there any longer. Then the men were allowed to go home and the King rode inland and the ships were sent to London and many perished before they came there."[12]

Harold disbands the Fyrd at the end of August or first week in September. I see a fast ship leaving England with the news and reaching William by end of that week.

William acted at once and moved to his advanced base at St. Valery between 8th-10th of September 1066. Again, he waited and again there are those who maintain he was waiting for the wind, but this simply cannot be so. Harald Hardrada had sailed from Norway at the end of August and after various stops on route by way of the Orkneys, and including harrying the coast of Scotland, arrived in England and entered the Humber estuary on or about the 18th or 19th of September. Some of the winds which favoured him would also have favoured William, though I have to admit that the Viking longboats were also propelled a great deal of the time by oars, which we are fairly certain was not the case with many of William's ships. More importantly is the fact that it is highly unlikely that a weather front against William would have lasted that long at that time of year. William was either awaiting confirmation that Hardrada had sailed, or deliberately allowed Hardrada to strike first and bear the brunt, so as to allow William to land unopposed.

Again, I feel that William had a spy in Harold's camp and that as soon as Harold got wind of Harald Hardrada's landing, and William learned of Harold's decision to go north, then William decided to sail. *Now* he would have to wait for the weather. He eventually sailed on 27th September 1066, two days after the battle of Stamford Bridge, but he does not yet know that. Is he going to face Harold Godwinsson or has Harald Hardrada, the greatest warrior of his day won, backed perhaps by Tostig? Or worse, still have the brothers Godwinsson come to an agreement and will he face the combined might of the two armies, West-Saxon and Dane/Norwegian? The die is cast and there is no turning back!

References: Chapter 4

1. McLynn, F. *op. cit.* Chapter 8, "Tostig."

2. According to Ebrard de Montgomery, or at least sources attributed to him, his father, Roger de Montgomery, commanded some 3,000 men on the right flank at Hastings, of which about 1,000 were mounted and about 300 were crossbowmen from the famous Bellême contingent. I have therefore extrapolated figures from these, but I believe they agree with most modern theories. See also Oman, C. Sir (1991 ed.) – *The History of the Art of War,* Vol. 1 p. 159, Greenhill Books, London, UK.

3. McLynn, F. *op. cit.* p. 193.

4. The Gokstadt ship excavated in Norway is 76.5 feet long and had a crew of 70. She is not particularly large, but provides an average.

5. McLynn, F. *op. cit.* p. 184.

6. Zukerman, A.J. (1972) – *A Jewish Princedom in Feudal France,* 768-900, p. 121-122, Columbia University Press, New York & London. See Genealogical Tree in Appendix. See also *The God Kings of Europe.*

7. McLynn, F. *op. cit.* p. 186.

8. Zuckerman, A.J. *op. cit.* p. 191.

9. Bartlett, R. (2000) – *England under the Normans and Angevin Kings* 1075-1225, p. 162, Clarendon Press, Oxford.

10. McLynn, F. *op. cit.* p. 192.

11. Bradbury, J. *op. cit.* p. 181.

12. Swanton, M. *op. cit.* p. 196, Abingdon Manuscript.

'*Chapter V*

What is a woman that you forsake her,
And the hearth-fire and the home-acre,
To go with the old grey Widow-maker?

(Harp song of the Dane Women from *Puck of Pook's Hill* by Rudyard
Kipling)

The Invasions

Most people regard the Norman Invasion as the only one that happened in
1066, but in point of fact, there were three invasions of England in that year.
The first was by Tostig, the brother of Harold Godwinsson, the second by
Harald Hardrada and Tostig combined and the third and only successful one
by William.

Tostig was the younger brother of Harold Godwinsson and had married
Judith, the sister of the Count of Flanders, and had been a firm favourite of
King Edward, who made him Earl of Northumbria. It was the first time that
an Anglo-Saxon and member of the powerful Godwin family had been given
a northern Earldom and it created considerable opposition on the part of the
northern magnates and particularly the Bamburgh family. This indeed shows
the divisions between the Danish families and the Anglo-Saxon ones. Edward
never really managed to integrate the two rival powers in his Kingdom.

Tostig is an interesting person in that he was apparently, like his mentor
Edward, particularly pious and appears to have been devoted to his wife,
unlike his brother Harold with all his mistresses. He was also determined to
bring justice to the north and reduce the powers of the local lords, who acted
more like bandits than nobles.

He also was probably encouraged by Edward, who perhaps saw him as his
successor.

Why he fell out with his brother Harold is uncertain, though I suspect that
Harold may well have already been plotting to seize England on Edward's
death and saw Tostig as a potential rival. Harold therefore did not support

55

his brother when the northern magnates rose in rebellion and demanded that Morcar replace Tostig as Earl of Northumbria.

When Edward died and Harold usurped the throne, he confirmed Morcar as Earl.

Tostig, who felt aggrieved at his treatment by his brother Harold, arrived at the Court of William in Normandy and requested help. Tostig's wife, Judith, was the aunt of Matilda, William's Duchess. William was sympathetic and realised that Tostig could help him, either by diverting Harold's attention and possibly inflicting damage on Harold's troops, or better still, could be instrumental in getting either Esthrithson or Hardrada to mount a joint effort and really weaken Harold for him. William sent Tostig with some help to his kinsman, the Count of Flanders, who apparently lent Tostig some vessels and presumably some money. At all events, Tostig sailed for Denmark, where he met with Sweyn Estrithson. Some authorities say he tried to convince Sweyn to help him and when this was unsuccessful, sailed for Norway and the Court of Harald Hardrada. I wonder, however, if he made an agreement between William and Sweyn that Sweyn would not claim the throne if William was successful. It certainly makes more sense. He then sailed for Norway.

It is far from clear what happened there, but apparently Tostig managed to overcome Harald Hardrada's initial rejection of the idea of an invasion and Harald agreed to call out his forces and to meet Tostig at the end of July or beginning of August, north of the Humber. Tostig then sailed back to Flanders where his second-in-command, Copsig, had assembled a fleet of at least 60 ships and men and from where he would have sent a messenger to William.

Tostig now launched the first of the three invasions in May, by attacking and capturing the Isle of Wight and forcing its inhabitants to provide food and money. From here he sailed for Sandwich, where he made another landfall and started to make a more permanent settlement. His brother, now King Harold, marched to Sandwich with his troops and Tostig's forces took to their ships and stood off the coast. To me, this "Invasion" was more of a probing raid to test Harold's defences and reactions and report back to William.

Tostig then decided to sail north, up to the Humber, where he tried to take over his old Earldom but was defeated by the Earls Morcar and Edwin. Morcar was the very Earl whose support by King Harold against Tostig had alienated Tostig and caused Tostig's thirst for revenge.

We know practically nothing of this battle, except that Tostig sailed into the Humber with 60 ships and sailed out with only 12, which means that one way or another Tostig had lost over 1000 men, which could have made all the difference had he kept them until Harold Hardrada arrived. Tostig then sailed north to take refuge with Malcolm of Scotland and await Hardrada.[40]

The second invasion was by Harald Hardrada. I have used the Scandinavian spelling "Harald" for Harald Hardrada and "Harold" for Harold Godwinsson or King Harold.

It is worthwhile to look quickly at the person of Harald Hardrada. I have devoted a complete chapter to him in *The God Kings of Europe*, so will merely give some basic information here. He was born Harald Sigurdsson and nearly lost his life in his first major battle when the forces of King Olaf Haraldsson, his half-brother, were annihilated at the battle of Stiklestad. Harald was rescued by one Rognvald Brusisson and was looked after by some peasants until his wounds had healed. Thereafter he made first for Kiev, where he found refuge with Prince Yaroslav, previously Grand Duke of Novgorod and the son of Vladimir Monakh, who had come to power with the help of Norse warriors.

Here Harald fought successfully against the Poles and East Wends, but then, according to the Sagas, asked for the hand of Elizabeth, the daughter of Yaroslav, when she became of marriageable age. Yaroslav was dismissive of this young warrior, saying that he must achieve fame and fortune before he could be considered as a suitable husband for Elizabeth. I suggested in *The God Kings* that Yaroslav may have made a bargain with Harald whereby should he obtain intelligence for Yaroslav, which would allow Yaroslav to sack Byzantium, then Harald would be rewarded with Elizabeth's hand. Harald therefore set out for Byzantium where he joined the famed Varangian Guard of Norse mercenaries.

Harald fought his way up from a Varangian mercenary to senior commander of the Imperial Varangian Guard and by 1042 had not only become a legend, but also had amassed an enormous fortune. How he got this fortune out of Byzantium is in itself an epic saga, but at all events, in 1043, Harald, together with a loyal following, escaped from Byzantium with his treasure and made his way through the Black Sea and then on to Kiev. It is not part of this book to go into the defeat of Yaroslav's fleet by the Byzantiums, but is sufficient to say that Harald married Elizabeth, thus making him a relation to many of the Royal Houses of Europe. Yaroslav's younger son married the Emperor Constantine's daughter, and Yaroslav's daughter Anna was married to King Henry of France (1031-60), and Anastasia to King Andrew of Hungary.

He was thus, at age 28, already the most famous warrior of his age. On his return to Norway, Harald persuaded his nephew Magnus that he should become joint King and upon Magnus's death, assumed the overall Kingship. As part of his consolidation of power he married Thora, daughter of the Arnmodling family head, Thorberg Arnesson of Giske, though still married to Elizabeth. Once again the sacred triangle, though polygamy was not unusual amongst the Vikings. This, then, was the second man who set sail to conquer England in August of 1066.

Again we do not know with any degree of certainty how large a force Harald had assembled, but best estimates would seem to put his fleet at between 200 to 500, so if we take an average of say 350 and multiply that by an average of 60 men per ship, then we have an invasion force of some of some 21,000 men, all of them warriors.[1]

This force is much larger than the force assembled by William, but there is one crucial difference. There may have been a few horses with Hardrada's force but even so, the warriors fought on foot, as did the Anglo-Saxon Housecarls.

Harald sailed first to the Shetland Isles and then on to the Orkneys where he left his first wife, Elizabeth, and their daughters, Maria and Ingigerd, in the care of the Orkney Islanders. His second wife, Thora, and their son Magnus, whom he appointed Regent in his absence, were left in Norway. It seems likely, therefore, that after conquering England, with or without William, he was going to transfer his seat of government to England or the Orkneys and leave Magnus as sub-king in Norway.

Besides Tostig, Harald had other allies – namely Paul and Erland, the sons of Thorfinn; also Godfrey, the son of Harald the Black, who joined him in the Orkneys. It must be remembered that Paul and Erland Thorfinnson were also distant cousins of William, being members of the Ulvungar dynasty.

They then sailed for England via Scotland and made their first landfall near Cleveland, where they sacked Scarborough. They also defeated a large force sent by the Earls Morcar and Edwin near to Holderness. They then sailed on until they entered the Humber estuary, where they met up with the remnants of Tostig's group.

Harald now anchored at Riccall and, leaving a strong guard in charge of Olaf and Eystein Orri, set out with Tostig to march to York. They presumably wished to repeat the success of Ragnald, who took York in 912 and reestablished the Viking kingdom of York, first founded by Halfdan, son of Ragnar Lothbrook (or Raghnaill) in 875. This was actually a very good strategy, as that part of England was still extremely loyal to the memory of Cnut's descendents and were anti the Godwin family. The problem was that Tostig himself was a Godwin and not exactly popular.

On the 20th September 1066 about half a mile from York, at Fulford Gate, Harald came upon the main strength of Edwin and Morcar, drawn up across the road with their right flank on the river and their left flank on a boundary ditch next to boggy ground. In this way they could not be outflanked. At first Edwin and Morcar's warriors met with success, but then Harald and his picked warriors smashed into the Saxons' right wing and after a ferocious hand-to-hand battle, the Saxons broke and fled. The slaughter that followed was devastating. Many Saxons drowned in the river Ouse or became trapped in the boggy ground that they had hoped to use to their advantage. The *Anglo-Saxon Chronicles* only say that Harald was victorious, but other authorities say that there were so many killed and drowned that the Danes were able to walk across the bodies as if on dry land.[2]

On the 24th September, York formally surrendered. Harald treated the town's inhabitants lightly and it seemed likely that he was ready to have himself crowned King of the old Danish Kingdom based at York.[3] It appears also that most of the Northern Counties at least tacitly supported Harald and indeed, it may well have been the fear of seeing his Kingdom divided that sent King Harold north by forced marches.

It must be assumed that Harold had been informed of Harald Hardrada's landfall at Riccall and his defeat of Edwin and Morcar's forces and I would assume that he had been informed of the submission of York on his way north as he arrived at Tadcaster late on September 24th.

Meanwhile, Hardrada had agreed to receive the submission of all the local magnates at Stamford Bridge, on the Derwent, a tributary of the Ouse, and had marched there from his camp at Riccall, where he had left all the booty and tributes he had collected and where he left the majority of his force to guard it, including Olaf, Paul and Erland Thorfinsson. He therefore only had with him a small force, perhaps 5,000 men in all, and they were lightly armed with only swords and bows; no mail or shields. Why Harald, who had trained in the Varangian Guard, should be so silly as to have his men only lightly armed and why his military intelligence did not inform him of Harold's approach is one of the major questions of history. On such chance happenings does the outcome of History depend.

It seems likely that Harold Godwinsson left Tadcaster at about 6 AM on 25th September, arriving in York early in the morning. We do not know how York received him, having made submission to Hardrada only the day before, but at all events they did not oppose him. Learning that Hardrada was to receive the submission of the local magnates at Stamford Bridge, Harold decided to march directly there, hoping to catch Harald and Tostig unawares.

Apparently, the first inkling that Hardrada had of Harold's approach was when he saw the dust of Harold's army over the brow of the hill. The *Sagas* recount the most wonderful series of verbal stand-offs, many of which I feel sure did not take place, though it is without doubt that some sort of pre-battle exchange would have happened. It is likely that Harold and a small body of Housecarls rode over to parley. It is also likely that Harold offered Tostig his Earldom back, as Edwin and Morcar were shown to be broken reeds. Tostig then asked what would happen to Hardrada and when Harold replied that Hardrada could only expect a grave, then Tostig turned his back on his brother and refused to betray Hardrada. It is interesting that Tostig is shown up as the perfect Knight and perhaps why King Edward had favoured him. McLynn even goes so far as to call him "sans peur et sans reproche."[4]

The battle was now joined, with the Danes defending the bridge, to try to deny the Saxons the opportunity of using their greater numbers until help could arrive from the vessels at Riccall. The story goes that one giant Norwegian defended the bridge almost on his own and killed over forty men with his battle axe until the Saxon's, tired of being denied the use of their greater numbers, sent a man with a spear under the bridge in a boat and stabbed the giant in the foot, whereupon he was overcome and the Saxons were able to rush the bridge. It was mid-afternoon by the time the Saxons could cross the bridge and engage the Danes in hand-to-hand combat.

Hardrada, epic poet to the last, dictates a short poem to his scribe:

> "We march forward in our battle hordes,
> Without our mail to meet dark swords,
> Though helmets shine,
> I have not mine,
> Our armour lies on our ships' boards." * (see notes)

Harald without helmet or mail soon met his death. An epic death for an epic warrior.

He was the last great Viking Warrior, who made his name in personal combat in the old way, on foot and with a poem on his lips. It is very difficult for a modern reader to appreciate just what the death of Harald Hardrada meant. He was a hero in the sense of Beowulf or the great Irish hero, Cuchulain. Rough yet gentle going into battle, knowing he will be slain, but going with a song on his lips. "How are the Mighty fallen in the midst of the Battle!"

At this point there was a lull in the battle and Harold offered terms to the Norsemen if they would surrender, but his brother Tostig showed the courage which made him *sans peur et sans reproche*. Taking his stand by Hardrada's standard, *Land-Ravager*, he defied his brother. His men gave a shout of defiance and the battle was joined again.

By all accounts, this second part of the battle was even bloodier than the first. Tostig himself was killed and most of his men slaughtered, but the Saxons themselves took heavy casualties. Indeed they almost lost the battle, for they were resting after what they had thought of as victory when they were attacked from their right wing by Eystein Orri, who had now arrived from Riccall with reinforcements.

As soon as the message reached Orri that Hardrada was under attack, his men donned their mail and with swords and shields set out to come to Hardrada's assistance. It took him, however, some 3 hours to reach the battlefield as he had to find a new approach and came via Catton to Stamford Bridge. Although tired by the march in sweltering heat, they charged upon the Saxons. This charge was to become famous as the "Storm of Orri" and very nearly succeeded in breaking Harold's line. The Saxons, however, rallied and fought the Norse to a standstill. This part of the battle lasted until nightfall, by which time Orri and all the other leaders were dead. Under cover of darkness the remaining Norse crept away and returned to their ships. Paul and Erland had evidently been left to guard the ships, as after the battle they returned to the Orkneys with Prince Olaf. Harold was left in possession of the field, but the cost to him in killed and wounded seriously weakened him for his encounter with Duke William.

By all accounts, Harold was in the middle of a victory celebration when the news was brought to him of William's landing. One can imagine the scene. Harold sitting in a high-backed chair, much like a throne, surrounded by his housecarls, all raising their drinking horns to him:

"Skall – the great warrior! Skall – the slayer of the great Hardrada! Skall – to the King!"

Suddenly a dusty and tired messenger enters the hall and falls to his knees at Harold's feet:

"Sire – The Norman's have landed."

There is a hush, as the men stop their boasting, to listen to the words of the messenger.

The carousing stops, though I suppose some warriors will have continued, but most will have realised there was to be no rest. Far from victory, they now have to face the third invasion, this time by the mail-clad horsemen of Duke William.

William's forces landed at Pevensey, on the coast, just south of Hastings, on 28th September 1066, three days after the battle of Stamford Bridge. The beach was undefended, as Harold had pulled his troops out of Pevensey to help him against Hardrada at Stamford Bridge. Pevensey was ideal for the landing. It had docks and fortifications since Roman times and William was able to land 3000 battle ready troops in a single afternoon.

At this point William still did not know whom he would have to face, but one assumes that he obtained information fairly quickly and prepared to meet Harold. He moved to Hastings and built a motte and bailey surround there. He would have known that he was on Harold's personal territory and deliberately set about harrying the countryside, burning down homesteads and forcing people from their homes, taking their livestock, etc. This had two distinct advantages. It meant that Harold would be faced with a whole tide of refugees that he would have to feed. It would reflect badly on him as a King, particularly because his private land was Wessex, and if he did not defend his people, it provided William with fresh meat and corn.

Harold, when told of this new threat, decided to move from York to London and arrived in London on 6th October. He left Edwin and Morcar, the defeated Earls, to try to get together as many men as possible and to join him in London. In London he took council and decided against the advice of his own brothers to march to Hastings and try to surprise William, just as he had surprised Hardrada.

Leofwine, his brother, had urged him to let him, Leofwine, lead their forces whilst Harold stayed behind to recruit more men and bring them up in support – or should Leofwine be overcome, at least Harold would have the chance of having a second crack at William.

But William had well judged Harold's temperament and had surmised that if he, William, caused enough havoc in Harold's own back yard then Harold would rush to the rescue; and so it proved. Harold decided on an all or nothing battle.

Harold gathered together all those troops he could muster in time. They consisted of his Housecarls, who it must be remembered had already fought what amounted to two battles, first against Hardrada and Tostig and then against Orri. They would have lost a great many of their number and many would have sustained wounds and they would all be tired. Besides these, there were the Thegns, who had answered Harold's call to meet him in London, and these included the Sheriffs and Abbots from Oxford and Kent. On his way south, Harold would have met up with the Fyrd from southern England and some from Norfolk and Suffolk, who had been summoned to meet him.

The most important troops were always the Housecarls, the permanent well-trained and well-armed troops of a King or magnate. The Thegns were the landowners who owed military service and again, would be well trained and well armed, and they in turn would be accompanied by their own housecarls. The Fyrd, although much larger in number, were basically men of military age with some military training and experience, but who were only called up to fight in emergencies and who could normally only be called up for a specific number of days per year; say 40. This then, was the force that Harold assembled to meet the Norman threat.

Harold decided to try to repeat his successful strategy against Hardrada and catch William unawares by force, by marching to Hastings. He arrived there on Friday 13th October, or possibly as late as 2 AM on the 14th, with an exhausted Army.

References: Chapter 5

1. See note 4, Chap. III, regarding Gokstadt excavation.

2. Swanton, M. *op. cit.* pp. 196-197; also McLynn, F. op. cit. p. 199.

3. Powicke, Sir F.M. & Fryde, E.B. (1961) – *Handbook of British Chronology*, 2nd. Edition, pp. 26-27, Royal Historical Society, London, UK.

4. McLynn, F. *op. cit.* p. 202.

* This translation is mine. I have tried to maintain the sense and stanzas of the original, as well as make the modern English rhyme in the same way as the original. I take full responsibility if this has not been achieved. This death poem is based upon one of the *Sagas* and it is probably a moot point as to whether Harald Hardrada actually dictated it. However, Harald was an extremely good poet and some of his poems still exist, including a beautiful one to his first wife Elizabeth – *The Princess of the Ring*. So it is possible.

Chapter VI

See you our stilly woods of oak,
And the dread ditch beside?
O that was where the Saxons broke,
On the day that Harold died!

(From Puck's Song – *Puck of Pook's Hill* by Rudyard Kipling)

The Battle of Hastings

For the sake of ease I have divided the battle into four phases, each with a subphase, though in reality I doubt that the participants would have recognised these phases.

In phase 1(a), the Saxons are detected by the Norman Scouts on Calbec Hill. This hill is about 2 miles north of Battle Hill and there is a good argument that Hastings actually took place here and not at Battle Hill, however, I do not intend to go into the arguments for and against in this book, but will assume, for the purposes of this book, that the battle took place on Battle Hill.[1]

Harold's men attempt to seize the high ground of Battle Hill. William sends archers, particularly crossbowmen, to intercept Harold. It would appear that many of the Fyrd had never faced crossbowmen before, because the force of the quarrels going through their shields and coats of mail, or more likely byrnies, was so terrifying that many apparently fled, calling out that the Normans had a secret weapon. The housecarls, however, were made of sterner stuff and gained the top of Battle Hill and held it so that the remainder of Harold's army could now join them. Harold's troops now dismounted to fight as the Vikings and Saxons had always done.

It seems likely that William now ordered the archers to harry Harold's forces whilst his cavalry armed themselves and mounted their destriers. The Saxons would have formed their famous shield wall, protected at the rear by a wood, which would stop William's troops from infiltrating them from the rear.

In his Roman de Rou, Wace says:

"Fait orent devant els escuz,
De fenestres et d'altres fuz,

65

> Devant els les orent levez,
> Comme cleies joinz e serrez,
> Fait en orent devant closture,
> Ni laissierent nule jointure."

However, if one changes "fenestres" for "fresnes tresses" (a simple copy error or indeed a change to scan), then one has a translation, which goes something like this:

"They made in front of them shields of wattled ash and of other woods, they raised them in front of themselves like hurdles joined and set close; they left no opening in them but made them into an enclosure."[2]

This has always seemed to me to be a wonderful description of a Saxon shield wall.

William now drew up his army with archers on each flank and infantry in the centre. Behind these were his main troops, his cavalry; Bretons on the left wing, under Count Alan Fergant, cousin of their ruling Count, together with men from Maine and Anjou, and those from Thouars under their Lord Aimeri. Normans, with William in the centre, were assisted by FitzOsbern. Mixed Flemish, Boulognaise and some Normans on the right wing, were under the command of Eustace of Boulogne and Roger de Montgomery, with the young de Beaumont in charge of some one thousand Beaumont troops.[3] It is not clear, from what accounts of the battle remain, as to whether there was now another advance of infantry and archers, or whether this was simply a continuation of the ongoing harrying process.

Phase 1(b) therefore, may well have been an ongoing part of phase 1(a). This was probably an advance by infantry and archers to "soften up" the shield wall and the defenders, but in order to understand the various tactics one must look at how the two hosts were organised. Let me say straight away that there can be no definite answer, but the following is likely from both the Bayeaux Tapestry and stories written after the battle, but within living memory of those who took part.

I tend to the position adopted by Sir Charles Oman. The front rank of Harold's force was composed of Fyrd on either side of the Thegns, and their housecarls in the centre, with probably Harold's brothers in command of the front centre, with Harold behind.

The Fyrd would, at most, have had byrnies – leather breast plates sewn with brass or iron. Many would have had only their working clothes and cloth headgear, armed with a motley array of swords, axes, spears or perhaps tools used for working the land and adapted to the role of war.

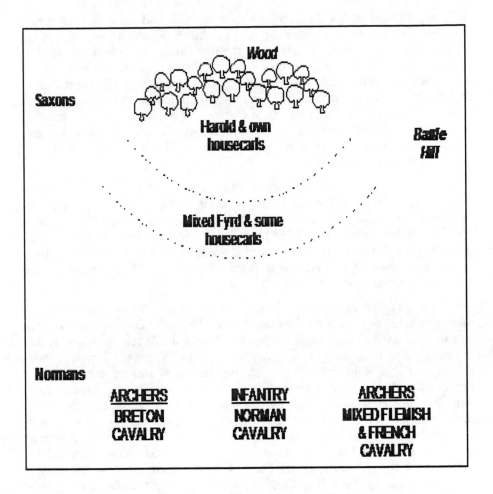

Fig. 7 - The Forces at the Battle of Hastings.

In phase 1(a), I have presumed a running battle as William's archers fought to stop Harold's men from obtaining the brow of the hill. In the second part, there would have been a more deliberate advance with the Norman infantry marching up the hill, covered by the archers and attempting to dislodge the Fyrd whilst they were still trying to form up. (4)   Jim Bradbury, in his *Battle of Hastings*, has suggested that Harold would have been in the front line, (5) but I would suggest that whilst his brothers may have been, he would have been the last line of defence under his dragon standard, (6) and possibly his own personal banner of the fighting man.

In his book, *Battle of Hastings*, Bradbury has suggested that the Normans were already on the march (the cavalry were already mounted) when they encountered Harold. My disagreement is that if that had been so, then surely William would have sent cavalry to take the hill position, not archers, as his cavalry would have arrived quicker at the brow than the infantry. Indeed, it is precisely one of the reasons for suggesting Calbec Hill as the place of the battle, and not Battle Hill. There is, however, another possibility and that is that the Norman and other cavalry were not mounted on their war horses or destriers, but on their riding horses or palfreys[7] and that it took time to bring up the destriers and charge. Though, William would, I would have thought, been too experienced a General not to have had at least some of his cavalry mounted and ready to engage.

I prefer, therefore, the contention that phase 1(b) was an advance by infantry and archers up the hill against a Saxon host who by now were partly assembled and ready for the attack. Ordericus says that the attack opened with an infantry attack, supported by archers, and I see no particular reason to doubt him. William, I think, hoped that the infantry attack, and particularly the archers, would open up cracks in the shield wall for his cavalry, but in that event he was disappointed.

Phase 2(a) now commences. This is the attack by mounted Knights and men-at-arms against an unbroken shield wall. From the Bayeaux tapestry we can see that most of the Knights appeared to have used their spears overhand to throw, rather than using them couched as a lance. Whether this was actually so we cannot be sure, but my gut feeling from a military point of view is that the cavalry were trying to achieve what the archers had failed to do, namely cause enough mayhem by throwing spears to allow the cavalry to drive through. The cavalry was at a considerable disadvantage, as they were charging uphill, so much of their velocity was lost. The ground was uneven with boggy earth and perhaps ditches in front of the Saxon line. "Senlac," the Saxon name for the battle, means Lake of Sand or perhaps Bog, and anyone who has toiled up this hill towards the crest on a wet October day, or who has taken part in a reinactment wearing chain mail and carrying a spear and a kite-shaped shield, will very soon realise that "Senlac" expresses the feel of the hill very well. Some confirmation that Battle Hill was indeed the same as "Senlac" comes from the name of a tract of land in the Battle Abbey's foundation called "Santlache."[8]

The cavalry were no more successful and eventually retreated.

Now begins what I have called phase 3(a). With the attack having petered out and the cavalry now obliged to fall back to regroup, the Saxon army advances. Indeed, they probably advanced some way as the Norman infantry came under attack and had to retreat, but again there is no reason to suppose that at that stage the infantry were not up there with the cavalry, slogging it out with the Saxons. It seems likely, however, that the retreat of the infantry caused problems for the Bretons on the left and perhaps with some of William's main Norman cavalry, though it is possible that the various wings and the centre were by now inextricably mixed. Phase 2 ends with the inability of the Normans to penetrate the shield wall and phase 3 begins with the Saxon advance.

As the Norman cavalry and infantry retreat, the Saxons advance. The Fyrd, less experienced and probably less disciplined than the housecarls, think perhaps that the Normans are in full retreat and run forward to attack, breaking away from the protection of the shield wall. The Normans, with their infantry now mixed with the cavalry, cannot retire easily to regroup behind their infantry, which is what should have happened. Instead, they have the Saxons snapping at their heels. It is possible that in this melee William is either unhorsed or his banner is cut down, for suddenly a cry goes up, "The Duke is dead!"

This is the crucial moment of the battle. If the Normans now retreat in earnest they have lost the day. The Bayeaux Tapestry shows William pushing back his helmet to show his face and shows Eustace of Boulogne pointing to him to rally the troops. My question here is what was Eustace of Boulogne, supposedly one of the leaders of the right wing, doing so close to William? Had the cavalry become so inexorably mixed that the leaders had lost control? Had Eustace ridden over to William to suggest a withdrawal? There is certainly some evidence for the latter view. Perhaps the leaders of the wings had ridden over to confer with William. We shall never know, but the question is intriguing! It is also possible that this is mere propaganda on the part of Odo when commissioning the Tapestry, to show his friend Eustace in a favourable light. Other authorities tend to suggest the opposite.

Bayeaux Tapestry Photo 3

The Battle of Hastings - Odo with a club - William lifts his helmet to show his face

Whatever the reason, the leaders manage to rally the cavalry and in phase 3(b) turn upon the Fyrd, who had rashly rushed forward and slaughtered them to a man.[9]

The end of phase 3 sees the Saxons considerably weakened and for the first time, Poitiers says, "gaps began to appear." The shield wall had effectively been breached in places.

Phase 4(a) is now a concerted effort by William and his Knights to keep up the pressure on the Saxon line. I suspect that this phase, from the point of view of the Normans, was the most costly in terms of men and horses killed. William had three horses killed under him. The right wing under the youngest Beaumont, taking part in his first battle, attacked with vigour and it is now that the feigned flight took place, when once again the Saxons were tempted out of their shield wall and which effectively led to the final defeat of the Saxons. To those historians who claim that feigned flight was not a tactic that was possible, I would point out that this had been used many times by the Normans (see Chap. 2, page 14).[10]

This time, Poitiers says, "a thousand men pursued the retreating Normans." But in this case, the Normans were in control of their flight. The right wing swung around behind the Saxons, thus cutting them off and surrounding them. The centre and left wing now turned to complete the encirclement and a massacre ensued.

A number of authors have pointed out that for this to happen, the right wing would have had to have their backs to the main Saxon line. Tactically, I don't see this as a problem. What I think happened is that the right wing hit the Saxons on their left flank. Some Saxons continued forward and were encircled, whilst others were able to retreat to the main Saxon line, pursued by part of the right wing. Thus, part of the right wing would have been keeping up the pressure on the main Saxon force, whilst the remainder would have been engaged in closing the circle.

At some stage in phase 4, Harold was killed, probably by an arrow. Again there are arguments about this, but I will go along with my reading of the Bayeaux Tapestry and that of David Bernstein and others. I am particularly impressed by the arguments of Sir Charles Oman in his seminal work, *The History of the Art of War in the Middle Ages*.

This work may be a little old now, first published in 1924, but I have yet to find better in terms of military knowledge of the period and real scholarship. However, as I pointed out in *The God-Kings of Europe*, Harold had to be shown to be killed in this way in order to make the Ulvungar "geas" come true. The whole business of Carmen is, I believe, an attempt by a romantic writer to have William fight and kill Harold personally, a sort of Lawrence Olivier, Henry V.

Interestingly, whilst searching documents in odd corners of Normandy, such as the libraries of Mayoral offices, I came across a note in a Genealogy of the Pontieu's that stated: Hugh de Pontieu – "Mort a Hastinges." There was nothing further, but perhaps Agnes did have a brother, who died at Hastings, which is why her husband, Robert de Bellême, inherited in her name.

Harold's brothers Leofwine and Gyrth probably died earlier in the battle, certainly this is how it is presented in the Bayeaux Tapestry, but once Harold had died, then the result was not in doubt. His housecarls would have fought on. They had a duty to protect their Lords' body or die with him. The remainder of the army who fought on hoped to gain the cover of night to get away. They did not manage it.

The critical moment apparently came at about 3 PM. After a further infantry attack, the cavalry made a final charge, which broke the shield wall. Once that happened there was no hope and the Saxons broke and fled. In the Bayeaux Tapestry, one can see archers at the bottom of the picture creeping up what appears to be a ditch in order to shoot at the Saxons from as near as possible. Although the Tapestry shows archers using what amounts to hunting bows, I suspect that most of them would have been crossbowmen. We know that the Bellême contingent were mostly crossbowmen and that they had had a devastating effect earlier on and I believe had a decisive effect at the end as well. I have called this stage 4(b), but as I mentioned at the beginning of this chapter, this is purely my way of trying to distinguish different parts of the battle. Other historians have divided the battle into other phases, but in point of fact, it is doubtful if the original participants would have recognised any of the phases. My own experience is that the average soldier has very little idea of what is going on generally and tends to concentrate on his own immediate problems and staying alive.

After the Saxons broke and fled, the Normans who could, pursued them and some apparently fell into a ditch, now called "Malfosse." Curiously, this gives further credence to the Calbec Hill theory mentioned earlier as a place named "Maufosse," just north of Calbec Hill, has been identified in certain medieval charters. It is possible that this was a fallback position, or "last ditch defence," or it may have been purely a fortuitous help to the Saxons. At all events, it cost many Normans dearly at the last moment. Thus ended the Battle of Hastings and with it the last time that the old Viking shield wall would be used against mail-clad cavalry.

Bayeaux Tapestry Photo 4
The Archers cause havoc and Harold's Army is defeated

That night William ordered his tent pitched on the crest of the hill. He was the victor of this battle but not yet King of England. Later he will command an Abbey to be built on the site, the ruins of which still exist to this day. The place of the high altar is supposed to be on the spot where Harold died. The problem is that we do not know if this is really the site or not. If, as some authors suggest, Calbec Hill was where the battle took place, then the Abbey is about two miles from where it should be.

The battle of Hastings was decisive against Harold but did not mean that William was automatically accepted throughout Edward the Confessor's Old Kingdom. It did mean that the vast majority of the Anglo-Saxon nobility of southern England was destroyed.

Of the leaders, only Esegar the Staller and Leofric, Abbot of Bourne, are recorded as escaping and they were grievously wounded.[11] The numbers of slain on both sides are unknown but so far as the Anglo-Saxons were concerned, virtually the whole of the Army perished. William rested his Army at Hastings until the 20th October and sent to Normandy for reinforcements. In the meantime, Archbishop Ealdred and the infamous Earls, Morcar and Edwin, persuaded the Witan to elect Edgar the Aethling as King.

From Hastings, William moved first to Romsey where he executed numbers of the populace for killing some of his men who had landed there earlier, by accident. From there he moved to Dover, which surrendered without a fight. Unfortunately, William's troops took matters into their own hands and gutted the place. Next, he moved on to Canterbury and then Winchester, though they very nearly didn't get that far, with William and many of his Knights going down with dysentery in Canterbury.

Eventually William moved to London, which he did not attack immediately, but rather laid waste the countryside around to ensure no supplies could get through. Finally, the Londoners and the remaining nobility, including the Saxon Edgar Aethling, made their submissions and begged William to take the crown. So there in London on Christmas day, 1066, William was crowned King. The invasion by the Norman families under William has been successful. Now the real business of conquest was to begin.

References: Chapter 6

1. For arguments regarding Calbec Hill as the place for the Battle of Hastings, see Bradbury, J. *op. cit.* pp. 168-176.

2. Oman, C. Sir (1991) – *A History of the Art of War in the Middle Ages*, Vol. 1, p. 155, Greenhill Books, London, UK.

3. Ibid. p. 159.

4. Ordericus Vitalis *op. cit.* p 184.

5. Bradbury, J. *op. cit.* p 184.

6. The Bayeaux Tapestry shows Harold with his Dragon standard, but his standard of the Fighting Man is said to have been sent to Rome as an offering after the battle. See also Bradbury, J. *op. cit.* p 178.

7. Bennett, M.(1988) – *Wace and Warfare* in Anglo-Norman Studies, XI pp. 37-58.

8. Oman, C. Sir *op. cit.* Vol. 1 p. 152 (note 2).

9. William of Poitiers *op. cit.*

10. See also Bradbury, J. *op. cit.* p 199.

11. Oman, C. Sir *op. cit.* Vol. 1 pp. 115 & 165.

Chapter VII

See you our little mill that clacks,
So busy by the brook?
She has ground her corn and paid her tax
Ever since Domesday Book.

(From Puck's Song – *Puck of Pook's Hill* by Rudyard Kipling)

Legal and Social Changes

In order to understand the changes that took place after the invasion and as a result of it, one must first look at the legal and social positions during the 24 years of Edward the Confessors' reign, as Harold's had been too short to have had any real impact.

According to an English Serjeant-at-Law, in 1470 the "Common Law" had been in existence since the creation of the world (Wallyng v Meger – (1470) – 47 SS 38 per Catesby Sjt.). He probably believed this statement, but we must look a little closer.

Mercia and Northumbria were under Danelaw, though according to Maurice Ashley there were differences even between Mercia and Northumbria and even further, local laws. This had been tempered somewhat during Edward's period. East Anglia and Wessex were under Anglo-Saxon law, which in many ways was similar to, but not identical with, Norman feudal law. Even in the *Leges Henrici Primi* (c. 1118) there was still the Law of Wessex, The Law of Mercia and the Danelaw, though each varied from place to place.[1] Normandy by contrast was under Carolingian feudal law, but with certain characteristics, which were particular to Normandy and probably inherited from Scandinavian sources. Under Danelaw, the King and great nobles could designate their successors, but land was held on behalf of the community or family. The warriors did not generally hold land but fought for the chief (the Giftgiver). Under Anglo-Saxon law there was an hereditary Monarchy, though confirmed by the Witan. Some of the great Earls held land in their own right and could pass it on to their sons, however there were specific cases of exception to this, Northumbria being one such.

Under Edward, the situation was gradually changing. Edward had spent his first 25 years living in Normandy, under the protection of the Norman Dukes, latterly under William himself. He had brought many Norman Barons and Knights with him and indeed they helped to keep him in power against the machinations of the Godwins. Edward had ruled England for 24 years (1042-1066). He was most at home with the feudal system and had undoubtedly made changes to both the Danelaw and Anglo-Saxon systems. It is not unreasonable, therefore, to say that to a degree the Feudal system was already operating in England.

William recognised this fact and very shrewdly proclaimed that the law was the same as that "upon the day on which King Edward was both King and dead." In other words, the law was identical to the last day of King Edward's reign.

This solution for William was very neat. It gave him a breathing space before having to make changes. It also importantly overcame any awkward decrees of Harold, which might have given him trouble. Implicitly, it meant that Harold's reign as King had never taken place. He, William, had been King from the moment of Edward's death. "King Edward is dead, long live King William." It also overcame any Anglo-Saxon objections. They could hardly complain if the law was the same as the last 24 years. It also meant that he did not have to worry about any differences between Danelaw and Anglo-Saxon law. If King Edward had changed Danelaw during his 24 years, then the changes had been Edward's, not William's.

It is exactly what modern politicians do – blame their predecessors for all the ills because of what they inherited, whilst taking credit for all the things that go right.

More than this, William could introduce changes and claim that they were merely to "clarify" Edward's laws. Courts today regularly change laws, claiming that they are merely "clarifying or interpreting" the laws made by Parliament – as Karr once said,

" Plus ça change, plus c'est la même chose."

At this point, I think it wise to mention the work of Prof. James Campbell, Professor of Medieval History at Oxford University. In his recent book *The Anglo Saxon State*,[2] Prof. Campbell is extremely critical of the work of Prof. Norman Davies's – *The Isles, A History*.[3] It is not my intention to enter into an argument on the merits or otherwise of either side in this debate. I have made my position clear at the beginning of this book. Readers who are interested should read the books for themselves and make up their own minds. As a general point, in this chapter I have tried to ignore both arguments and have, by and large, relied upon my own research and opinion.

It must be remembered that prior to the Norman Conquest, England had neither legislature nor judicature in any developed sense. The Laws of Wihtred (c. 700 AD) were the result of a clerical assembly and reflect clerical rather than lay jurisprudence. Recent research has shown that the Laws of Aethelberht I of Kent may have been the last laws of a pagan King, but it is clear that the Anglo-Saxons did not codify laws, but rather gave guidance on matters that had hitherto been matters of discretion. The very word "Law" seems to have been imported from Denmark, whilst under the Anglo-Saxons it was known as "Folcriht," or communal justice.[4]

Let us therefore now look at the Feudal system in outline, a system which was gradually introduced by Edward and his Norman successors. The first point to mention is that the idea of freehold (or allodial), as we understand it today, did not exist. All land was the King's. The King then hands out land to his chief magnates to be held as "Tenants-in-chief." They in turn might hand some of this land to their supporters as "Tenants," and there might be sub-tenants as well. This process is called, in legal terms, "subinfeudation."[5] The land is held at the King's pleasure and may be taken away at any time. In practice, Kings did not do this very often or they would cause rebellion. It was also a method to earn the loyalty of their main supporters. Land was held on the basis of Military Service. Thus land is frequently described as "supporting one Knight" or more. Land able to support one Knight was called a "Knight's fee" and a manor of a Baron would normally consist of several "Knight fees," depending upon how important the Baron was. Earls at the top of the range under the King (there were no other Dukes or Marquises at this point in England, after all, William, even as King of England, was still only Duke of Normandy) would have had both Barons and Knights as tenants and there were exceptionally Earls Palatine. Tenants-in-Chief taxed their own tenants who, in turn, taxed their own holdings. Tax was often in kind – for example food, beer, grain or services. Thus, someone might have to work so many days per month on his Lord's land instead of paying money. Tenants-in-Chief were responsible to the King for the taxes raised on their holdings and were responsible for not only collecting the taxes, but delivering the taxes to the King's exchequer. The Domesday Book, a great survey of England under William, was very much a practical tax roll. Its purpose was to find out how much revenue William could raise from his new Kingdom. Whether such systems existed on the continent on this scale is open to question. If they did exist, then none have survived to the same extent, though there is evidence from Flanders of a fragment of a pipe roll from 1140 and a "Groote Brief" from 1187.[6]

That an accounting system of some sort existed in the England of Edward the Confessor is without question, because Domesday makes this clear. Witness, for example, the entry for Olnay in Buckinghamshire: "in total value £12; when acquired £7; before 1066 £12."[7] There are many such entries, which clearly proves that an accounting system prior to 1066 existed. The problem is not that one existed, but when did it come into existence and was it representative of a European system or peculiar to England?

It must also be pointed out that holdings of major magnates tended to be dispersed around the country rather than concentrated in one place. There were a number of good practical reasons for this. First, both the King and his Barons lived peripatetic lives, as they literally had to eat their way around their holdings. This meant, hopefully, that a bad harvest in one place would not mean that the Lord and his tenants starved, but could receive food from another holding. It also probably meant that a Lord had a more varied diet, as what he ate in, say, Buckinghamshire, would be different to what he ate in Kent. It also meant that whilst the Knights, who moved around with their Lords, received likewise a varied diet, the peasant who was restricted to a small area within walking distance had much less variation in his diet. It also meant that it was more difficult for the Great Barons to forment rebellion. Their next-door neighbour might not agree. The exceptions to this were the so-called Earls Palatine. Those Earls were in charge of dangerous border areas like the Welsh and Scottish borders, or the coast. They needed, for defensive purposes, to have land and Knights concentrated under their control, so that quick action could be taken in case of unfriendly incursions.

These Earls Palatine tended, therefore, to be those closest to William in terms of blood. People who had helped him in the Conquest and whom he felt he could trust: Montgomery, Clare, Eu, Beaumont, FitzOsborn, Avranches, Mortain, Bayeaux, Tosny and Gifford, though sometimes that trust was misplaced. Roger de Montgomery, for example, besides holding much of the Welsh borders based on Shrewsbury, also held the Lewes rape; the Count of Mortain held Pevensey; whilst the Count of Eu held Hastings.[8]

The Conquest, like the Invasion before it, was very much a family affair. They married into each other's families and formed and reformed alliances over and over again. Indeed they continued to do so right up to the beginning of the 19th Century. In fact, many marriages were either banned by various Popes or the couple had to obtain special dispensation.[9]

There is considerable difference of opinion between scholars regarding the social changes that took place after the Invasion. George Garrett is a good example of those who maintain that a great deal of social change took place. He writes, "Those Barons whether ecclesiastical or lay held their lands precariously as tenants-in-chief quite differently from the Anglo-Saxon Thegn, who had a legally defined status and did not necessarily hold anything of the King."[10]

On the other hand, there is Prof. Frank McLynn, whom I have quoted extensively elsewhere, who wrote, "The same fundamental socio-economic system prevailed both in England and Normandy."[11] I have already mentioned the fact that the Confessor was in many ways more Norman than Anglo-Saxon and that he had already introduced a measure of feudalism into England prior to the Conquest, but it is worth while to look at the heirachial structure of the social order under Edward and William. Fig. 7 shows the outline structure at the time of the Confessor. There were very few Earls, who were the highest rank of nobility after the King. Often they were minor Kings leading the old independent Kingdoms of Mercia, Northumbria or Wessex. Under the King there were the "King's Thegns," who held their land directly from the King in return for military or civil service.[12] Then there were what I have called the non-royal Thegns, who held their land from another lord – either an Earl or another Thegn. A Thegn was by definition "someone who held enough land not to have to farm it himself."[13]

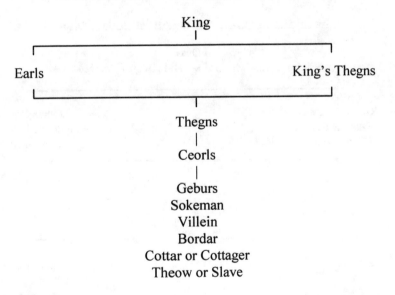

Social Structure under Edward the Confessor

King

Earls   King's Thegns

Thegns

Ceorls

Geburs
Sokeman
Villein
Bordar
Cottar or Cottager
Theow or Slave

Fig. 8

A Ceorl (pronounced "Churl") was a non-noble, usually a prosperous peasant who aspired to become a Thegn and could achieve this by acquiring five "Hides" of land (= 600 acres), or by deed or gift from the King or an Earl. This was in fact not that uncommon. A Gebur was a kind of middle peasant burdened by dues and rents. On the other hand, a Sokeman was an upper peasant owing only light service or sometimes none at all. In many cases, Sokemen were better off than some of the poorer Thegns.

A villein held anything from 15 acres to a full hide (120 acres), and although the name today is a substitute for criminal, in the 10th and 11th centuries a Villein was a much respected member of society. Just below the Villein in land holding was the Bordar, who held anything up to 15 acres, whilst the Cottar or Cottager was limited to a cottage. It is an interesting thought that the vast majority of people who own their thatched cottages or town houses would have been regarded in the 11th century as the bottom of the social scale. A Theow was the Anglo-Saxon slave, but he could only be bought or sold by a lord, a member of the Nobility. Slavery in Anglo-Saxon England was a legal punishment, usually for the inability to pay fines, but was limited to a specific period, presumably the period calculated to pay off the fine. A Housecarl might be a Thegn and was generally held to be of the thegnage class, though unless specifically a Thegn, was paid for his service by the King or Earl. Fig. 8 shows the social structure of Normandy prior to the Conquest of England, and Fig. 9 shows the social structure of England after the Conquest.

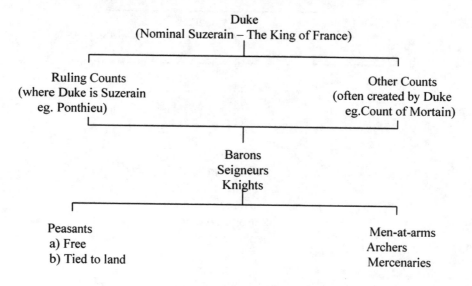

Social structure in Normandy prior to the Conquest

Duke
(Nominal Suzerain – The King of France)

Ruling Counts
(where Duke is Suzerain
eg. Ponthieu)

Other Counts
(often created by Duke
eg. Count of Mortain)

Barons
Seigneurs
Knights

Peasants
a) Free
b) Tied to land

Men-at-arms
Archers
Mercenaries

Fig. 9

Social structure of England after the Conquest

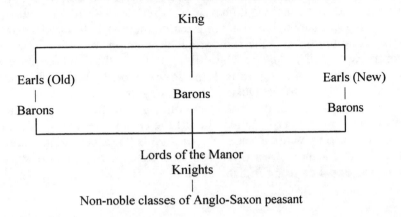

Fig. 10

At the top therefore, after the Conquest, you had a new King but no real changes; at the next level, that of Earl, there was again only change from Anglo-Saxon to Norman, and only then sometimes, but there were many new creations and they now fulfilled more exactly the equivalent of Norman Counts, with the Earls Palatine having a similar position to the old ruling Thegns. The Barons were really only a change in name. They were equivalent of the Thegns and indeed, several Thegns became Barons. The smaller Thegns became "Lords of the Manor," a new name for the smaller Thegn holdings, equivalent to the Norman Seigneurs. Many of these Lords of the Manor were to reward the poorest Knights or mercenaries, who had supported William or were given to each Earl or Baron, so that they in turn could reward their own supporters. The household Knight replaced the housecarl, becoming a dependent Knight in the household of the King, an Earl, Baron or Lord of the Manor.

The Anglo-Saxon Ceorls disappeared within a generation, either to become Knights, Lords of the Manor or descending down the social scale. The Sokemen continued until the 1200's, but gradually disappeared as well, whilst the difference between Villein and Bordar disappeared, both becoming known as Villeins. The Cottager remained until the 20th century and the Theow was replaced by the peasant, tied to the land. What we see therefore is a replacement of the top echelons of the nobility with Normans, particularly as I shall show in a moment, by William's kinsmen, but little real difference in the remainder of the social classes. The towns by and large retained their Charters and freedoms, and the peasants still ploughed the same fields. Changes did occur, it would be strange if they did not, but it was mostly gradual.

In the towns, the other change that would have been noticeable would have been the Jewish communities. I have mentioned the warriors of Septimania in Chapter II, but without the business acumen of the Jews it is doubtful if William's new Kingdom would have recovered or regained its wealth quite so quickly. No wonder the Norman kings called them "His Jews." The size of the Jewish communities and their importance is demonstrated by the ritual bath recently excavated in London (Daily Telegraph 25/10/01 and see photograph). There is another in Bristol. In fact, the Jews enabled the King of England to pay to his brother, Robert Duke of Normandy, the amount for which Robert had mortgaged his Duchy, so that he could go on the Crusade. Indeed, the Jews remained a power in England until the end of the reign of the Norman Kings. It was only with the accession of the Plantagenets and the marriage of Edward I to Eleanor of Castille, who was vehemently anti-Jewish, that the Jews were expelled from England in 1290.

Jewish Ritual Bath excavated in London and dated to 1066

Under the Confessor, the Thegns were still by and large a heterogeneous group of noblemen. The royal Thegns had held their land provisionally (not freehold), similar to the feudal system.[14] Their land was subject to "Geld," a cross between a tax and a mortgage. If you could not pay the tax then you might have to sell the land to pay off the "Geld." No transaction could be made without the King's specific "written" permission. A general agreement was not sufficient. Succession was subject to tax (eg. Death Duties or Inheritance tax, which was abolished by Magna Carta, and was not reintroduced, on a permenant basis, until the Labour government after the 2nd World War). Under William, the social structure became at once more defined and yet in many ways more flexible. He needed a defined social structure to control his new Kingdom, but also needed to be flexible, partly to accommodate the new lower ranges of the introduced aristocracy, but also to accommodate the established Anglo-Saxon magnates, who survived and now supported him.

Land holdings were now the same for all social groups. The Allod or family holding disappeared to be replaced with the true feudal holding. Land was subject to a "Service" tax, which was basically what Domesday was all about. The successor must do "homage." In other words a son, on inheriting, must attend the King at court and kneeling, place his hands between the King's, promising to be "His Man." However, land could also be acquired by marriage and if you were a border Baron then any new lands you conquered became yours.

I do not think that the effective legal system changed much. There were now Manorial Courts, Baronial or County (Earls) Courts and the King's Court. The Manorial Court could try any cases of wrongdoing on the land of the Manor. If a wrong was committed by someone from another Manor, then that lord would be given the opportunity to recover the offender and deal with the offender himself. Disputes between Manors could be referred to the Baron or Earl who, as Tenant-in-Chief, held both Manors, but where the Manors were held from differing lords then the dispute might be referred to the King's court. There was also the "Writ of Praemunire," whereby a case could be transferred to the King's court. Edward had started to use this more often than his predecessors and William and his successors followed suit. The other main change was the formalisation of the tax assessment system. The great Pipe Rolls, known as the Domesday Books, were to enable William to calculate the worth of his Kingdom for tax purposes. He sent commissioners to all countries to count acreage, livestock, ploughs, habitations, and to calculate what that bit of land was now worth. Every Manor was assessed. It has to be said that the Anglo-Saxons and particularly the clergy disliked it intensely, but then who likes paying tax? The tax was assessed by the Crown's Commissioners for the first time. Today we still have commissioners of tax, whose duty it is to assess our tax.

Two examples from Domesday must suffice to show how detailed they were. The first is from what is now Lyme Regis (in Dorset): "The Bishop of Salisbury holds Lym. Land for 1 plough. It has never paid tax. Fishermen hold it; they pay 15 shillings to the monks (of Sherborne) for fish. Meadow, 4 acres. The Bishop has one house there which pays 6 pence." You can see why the clergy disliked it, as they had never paid tax. The second is from Clun (in Shropshire): "Picot holds Clun from Earl Roger. (Roger Montgomery, Earl of Shrewsbury). Edric held it; he held it as a freeman (ie. Not for military service). 15 hides which pay tax. Land for 60 ploughs. In Lordship 2: five slaves; 10 villagers and four smallholders with five ploughs. A mill which serves the court; four Welshmen pay 2 shillings and 4 pence. Of this land Walter holds two hides from Picot; Picot, a man-at-arms three hides; Gishold two hides. They have three ploughs and two slaves; two ploughmen; eight villagers, four smallholders and two Welshmen with two ploughs between them. Two riders pay two cattle in dues. Value of the whole manor before 1066 £25; later £3; Now, of what Picot has £6 5s; of what the man-at-arms have £4 less 5 shillings." This one is interesting in that it shows clearly the points I have made. The tenant-in-chief is Earl Roger de Montgomery. The tenant or lord of the manor is Picot. Edric, an Anglo-Saxon, had held it previously (and was either dead or dispossessed), but whilst as Edric had held it "free of service," Picot has clearly to render service for it. The mill serves the manor or possibly the Earl's court. There are however some tenants who presumably had been there before, eg. Two Welshmen, but there are also some new ones. Men-at-arms serving Picot – one of them is also called Picot and is specified as a man-at-arms, to distinguish him from the lord of the manor, Gishold and Walter. The value of the manor had fluctuated. This part of the country was in very poor shape in 1068. The value had been £25, and had then dropped to as low as £3 and had now regained something, being now worth £10.

To someone visiting England in say, 1065 and again, in say 1076, the main noticeable difference would have been the castles. In the Confessor's England there were walled towns, but few if any castles. But within 10 years castles, first Motte and Bailey, then in stone, were being built all over England. The White Tower of the Tower of London is but one of the many built by William and his Barons to control the newly acquired lands. In fact, the number of Normans and other continentals settling in England was relatively small, and the top dogs were all family. If you look at the tenants-in-chief from Domesday you can see all the same names occurring over and over again, whether ecclesiastical or lay, but it is particularly noticeable in those areas along the coast or the borders with Wales and Scotland.

For example, in Cumberland and Yorkshire the main holders are: The King, The Archbishop of York; Robert, Count of Mortain; Count Alan of Brittany; Ilbert de Lacy. In Cheshire it is divided mostly between the Bishop of Chester and Hugh d'Avranches, now Earl of Chester (known as either the Wolf for his ferocity against the Welsh or the Fat, for his obesity).

In Shropshire, Roger de Montgomery is an Earl Palatine. He has castles at Shrewsbury, Montgomery (named after himself), Oswestry, as well as the Marcher lordships of Clun and Laidlow. His son Philip holds the manor of Wenlock near to Shrewsbury. His son Roger of Poictiers or Poitou, becomes Earl of Lancaster and Kendal and his son Arnulph, Earl of Pembroke. His son Hugh is made Earl of Arundel and later inherits his father's Earldom of Shrewsbury as well. His elder son, Robert, is Count of Bellême in his father's lifetime and later ruling Count of Ponthieu, through his wife Agnes. On his younger brother's death he also inherits the Earldom of Shrewsbury.

In Herefordshire there was already a Norman Baron, Alfred of Marlborough, who was one of the Confessor's Norman Barons, but just to be on the safe side, William FitzOsbern was made Earl of Hereford. In Kent his half-brother Odo of Bayeaux was made Earl of Kent, with Richard FitzGilbert's castle at Tonbridge and Hugh de Montfort's at Saltwood.

Sussex is particularly interesting. William took very careful precautions here to make certain no one else could mount a similar invasion to his. Sussex was therefore divided into five "Rapes" which were in parallel strips running from the coast to the county's northern border. Each rape was given to a powerful Norman Baron related by blood or marriage to William. William de Warenne held the rape of Lewes, William de Broase held the Bamber rape, whilst Roger de Montgomery held Arundel, the Count of Mortain the Pevensey rape and the Count of Eu held Hastings. Furthermore, each had to have mottes in depth, such as Verdley, Pulborough, Knepp, Channelbrook, Caburn and Burglow.

In Hampshire the King was the main land holder, whilst in Dorset Osmond of Sees (in Normandy) became Bishop of Salisbury, a member of the Privy Council and Earl of Dorset and Somerset. In Devon, besides the King, we find once again the Count of Mortain, Earl Hugh and the Bishop of Coutances and in Westmoreland it is again the King and Roger of Poitou (son of Roger de Montgomery).

References: Chapter 7

1. Baker, J.H. (1981) – *An Introduction to English Legal History* (2nd Edition), p. 12, Butterworth & Co. Ltd., London, UK.

2. Campbell, J. (2000) – *The Anglo-Saxon State,* p. ix, Hambledon and London, London & New York.

3. Davies, N. (1999) – *The Isles: A History*, Macmillan, London, UK.

4. Campbell, J. (2000) – *The Anglo-Saxon State*, p. ix, Hambledon and London, London & New York.

5. Baker, J.H. *op. cit.* pp. 1,2,3 & 195.

6. Campbell, J. *op. cit.* p xix.

7. *The Domesday Book* (1985) – Phoebe Phillips Edition, edited by Thomas Hinde, Hutchinson Ltd, London.

8. Ibid – Sussex.

9. Montgomery, H. (1992) *op. cit.* pp. 1,3,10,11 etc.

10. Garrett, G. – *Conquered England 1066-1215* an Illustrated History of Medieval England, Saul, N. (ed.), Oxford University Press, UK.

11. McLynn, F. *op cit.*

12. Campbell, J. *op cit.* pp 216-217.

13. Montgomery, H. – *Lectures on the Norman Invasion 1066*, given at University of Applied Sciences, Belgrade in 2000.

14. For more detailed analysis of the Anglo-Saxon and Norman land system and taxation see: *"Illustrated History of Medieval England,"* in various essays, *"The Oxford Illustrated History of Medieval Europe,"* essay The lineaments of power, *"The Anglo-Saxon State"* by James Campbell, the *"Domesday Book"* Ed. Thomas Hinde, and *The Isles: A History*, by N. Davies.

See also Hicks, C. – *England in the Eleventh Century,* Stamford Press, USA.

I have referred to the book by Maurice Ashley also in the text. This is *The Life and Times of William I* (1992) – Weidenfeld & Nicholson Ltd. UK.

Chapter VIII

"Clare has risen, FitzOsborne has risen, Montgomery has risen."

(From *Puck of Pook's Hill* by Rudyard Kipling)

Post 1066, the Domesday Book and the Families

Although William was crowned and acknowledged as King in the winter of 1066, it was to be another 20 years before England could be considered to be entirely under his control. In March of 1067 William returned to Normandy. He took with him as hostages Prince Edgar, as well as the Earls Morcar, Edwin and Waltheof, so as to remove any leaders of an Anglo-Saxon revolt. In his absence he appointed as joint regents Odo, Bishop of Bayeaux, now Earl of Kent and William Fitz Osbern, now Earl of Hereford. Their particular task was to fortify England by building castles throughout William's and their domains. Naturally, this was seen by the Anglo-Saxons as oppression. Anglo-Saxon chronicle says, "They built castles far and wide throughout the land, oppressing the unhappy people."

It was perfectly obvious however, to the Normans, that if they were to control England, they had to have castles in strategic places, just as they had in Normandy and the regents were obliged to set aside the objections of the people, who were either displaced or forced to work on these castles. There were of course revolts. The first was led by an extraordinary character called Edric the Wild, who was said by the Celts to have married a fairy.[1] This attack was aimed at the newly built Norman castle at Hereford, the northern base of William Fitz Osbern. Edric and his Welsh company failed miserably in their attack and instead laid waste and robbed the surrounding countryside before returning to Wales with the spoils.

I mentioned earlier that Eustace of Boulogne had tried himself for the Crown in 1051, and he now made another attempt. Apparently the people of Kent invited Eustace over, but it has always, to me, seemed to smell of something more. Odo of Bayeaux who was charged with the defence of

Kent, as Earl of the same, was conveniently away in the North when Eustace landed and therefore would not afterwards to be called to account by William. Eustace and his men meanwhile occupied the town of Dover, but the men of the castle garrison defended the castle stoutly and Eustace had to retire.

At the same time, the Northumbrians made overtures to Sweyn Estrithson, King of Denmark, with whom William had previously done a deal. William decided it was time to return and landed back in England on 6th December 1067. The first thing he did on his return was to lead a combined Norman and Anglo-Saxon army into Devon and Cornwall. He laid siege to Exeter, the capital of Devon, which resisted him for some 18 days. Surprisingly, King William allowed the city to surrender on terms, possibly because he felt that the revolt had been led by Harold Godwinsson's mother and his illegitimate sons, but who deserted the people of Exeter before the siege had finished. At all events, William ordered a castle to be built there and left a garrison to secure the area. The revolt must have been quite well supported, as William had to deal with both Bristol and Gloucester shortly thereafter and again ordered castles to be built there.

At Whitsun in 1068 he decided that it was safe enough to bring over Matilda and had her crowned Queen, in Westminster Abbey. But although the South of England was firmly under Norman control, the North was not yet subdued. When William returned he brought back his hostages with him. Edgar escaped and fled north to the court of his brother-in-law, King Malcolm of Scotland. At the same time, the Northumbrians decided on rebellion, led by both their former Earl Morcar and their present Earl Gospatric, who was of Saxon noble blood and a friend of the dead Tostig.

The Northumbrians now sought aid from both Sweyn of Denmark and Malcolm of Scotland. William decided that the time had come to deal with these northern rebels once and for all. He went first to Warwick and then to Nottingham, both of which quickly submitted, and William was then able to enter York unopposed. The local lords swore fealty and Malcolm sent a message promising not to invade. William returned to London via Lincoln, Huntingdon and Cambridge. In all of these places he ordered castles to be built. He also sent a Norman, again family, Robert de Commines to Northumbria as its new Earl. He spent Christmas of 1068 in London.

If William thought that he had succeeded in taming the North he was sadly mistaken. The Northerners regarded William's relative leniency as a weakness. In January of 1069 the new Earl, Robert of Northumbria, was burnt to death in the Bishop's palace in Durham along with some 900 of his men.[2] In York the Norman commander of the castle was killed and Prince Edgar arrived from Scotland, to be welcomed by all the local magnates. Simultaneously, two of Harold's sons raided the south-west coast. William moved with speed. He rode north with almost his entire army and overwhelmed the rebels at York, slaying several hundred. This time there was to be no leniency. York was turned over to the plunder and rape of his soldiers. Edgar of course retreated to Scotland.

At the same time as William was dealing with the northern uprising, his local Norman commanders in Dorset, Somerset and Shropshire on the Welsh border, had to deal with attacks of their own. These commanders were not taken unawares, however, and were able not only to hold their own, but decisively defeat the rebel forces, although Shrewsbury itself was severely damaged by fire. These rebellions were mere diversions, however, compared to the attack that now took place. Sweyn Estrithson, King of Denmark, decided to try to gain the throne for himself and sent over a fleet under two of his sons and his brother.[3] Although this fleet was in fact smaller than that of Harold Hardrada in 1066, it was joined by all the local magnates around York, including Prince Edgar (who slunk south again), the disposed Earl Gospatric and this time, Earl Waltheorf.[4] York fell on 20th September 1069, to the Danes. Once more, William himself took control, moving north to force the Danes out of Lincolnshire, then suddenly turning west, he dealt effectively with another uprising by Edric the Wild. From there he moved in to the Midlands and, basing himself in Nottingham, started a systematic devastation of the northern counties. This policy was principally to deprive the Danes of supplies. After several delays he finally took York and decided to stay there to celebrate Christmas and to try to carry on a winter campaign, which certainly disconcerted his enemies. He forced his way across the Pennines and occupied Chester, as well as taking Stafford. Prince Edgar once again withdrew to Scotland and Earl Waltheof made his peace with the King. He was finally brought to book by plotting rebellion again, coupled with the machinations of his wife (see Chapter 2). Prof. Douglas states that the campaign of 1069 to 1070 "must rank as one of the outstanding military achievements of the age." To the Anglo-Saxon chronicler it was a disaster – "The King had all the monasteries in England plundered and in the same year there was a great famine." Obviously, William was not overly fond of the Church!

At Easter William finally reached Winchester and disbanded part of his army, paying off most of his mercenaries. All was not at an end, however. In the spring of 1070 King Sweyn himself arrived in the Humber with additional ships. They occupied the Isle of Ely and sacked Peterborough. Here they were joined by the most turncoat of Earls, Morcar and Edwin, plus a mysterious character called Hereward the Wake. This time William used diplomacy. He signed a peace treaty with Sweyn, who returned to Denmark full of booty. Morcar was taken prisoner and died in prison, whilst his brother Edwin was killed by his own followers while attempting to flee, once again, to Scotland. It seems that their followers had eventually realised that Edwin and Morcar were not interested in England, but only their own thwarted ambitions. Thus ended two rather unpleasant Anglo-Saxon Earls. William then headed himself for Ely where the rebels surrendered, but the person of Hereward escaped and disappeared from history to become mere myth.

The subjugation of England was now complete and the establishment of Earls Palatine mentioned in chapter VI worked reasonably well, in securing the borders. Although rebellions continued from time to time, including rebellions amongst the Normans, by and large the real conquest was over by the end of 1070. In 1085 King Cnut of Denmark and Olaf of Norway gathered together a large fleet to invade. The invasion did not materialise, but it made William realise that he needed to know how much tax was available to him in case of war.

In 1085 William held court at Christmas in Gloucester and the Anglo-Saxon chronicler says, "had much thought and very deep discussion about this country... Then he sent his men all over England into every shire... So very narrowly did he have it investigated, that there was no single hide nor a yard of land, nor indeed (it is a shame to relate but it seemed no shame to him to do) one ox nor one cow nor one pig which was there left out, and not put down in his record."

The Anglo-Saxons and indeed many of the Normans were horrified by his thoroughness. They could no longer escape their full tax quota, and there was real fear in the naming of the survey "Domesday" — The fear of the Day of Judgement.[5]

Rupert, Bishop of Hereford, in his description of the survey made it plain that not only did the commissioners make an original assessment, but that others from a different county were sent afterwards to check out the accuracy of the first commissioners. "After these investigations came others, who were sent to unfamiliar counties to check the first descriptions and to denounce any wrong doers to the King." William knew human nature and knew that some of his commissioners were not above taking a little bribe.

The Domesday Book clearly shows the feudal system at work. The land as a whole is deemed to be the King's. First are described the Royal manors and lands, then those of the Tenants-in-chief, both ecclesiastical and lay, then the sub-tenants of the Tenants-in-chief, then those holding from a sub-tenant, etc., all the way down the line. William himself did not live to see Domesday completed, dying in 1087 whilst campaigning against the French in Nantes.

Already during his lifetime William had faced rebellions against him from the Norman families. Roger of Breteuil, the son of his cousin and steward William Fitz Osborn, who had been created Earl of Hereford, became embroiled in a conspiracy against William in 1071 and was blinded and thrown into prison, where he died. Roger de Montgomery himself threatened rebellion, but was quickly brought to reason by William, and both Odo of Bayeaux and Eustace of Boulogne had tried unsuccessfully to raise the standard of rebellion. Already in August of 1086, William was beset by problems. Although the threat of invasion had receded, Philip of France was preparing an attack on Normandy, aided and abetted by Robert, William's eldest son. Odo of Bayeaux, his half brother, was confined to prison in Rouen but could still stir up trouble. William therefore decided to invoke a personal oath of loyalty from all those who had benefited from his English conquest and therefore, on 1st August 1086, William assembled all his tenants-in-chief and their military tenants or "peers of honour" on Salisbury plain and had them swear a personal "oath of allegiance."[6]

With the death of William, however, and the break up of his Anglo-Norman Kingdom, the alliances were stretched too far and a break up of the families of the conquest seemed inevitable. Rightly or wrongly, William decided to divide his Dukedom of Normandy and his Kingdom of England. He gave Robert, known as Curthose, his Duchy of Normandy and his son William, known as Rufus, his Kingdom of England. To those Norman magnates who owned land on both sides of the Channel, this was a far from ideal situation. Many like Robert de Bellême sided with Robert Curthose, whilst others took the side of William. Odo of Bayeaux rebelled within a year of William's death and was banished from England, his estate in Kent being forfeit.

It was not until the succession of Henry I that England and Normandy were united once again and William's legacy could be put on a firm footing. Once again, this did not outlast Henry's reign and with his death, England was plunged into civil war. The Ulvungar ambition, however, was to survive and with the marriage of Henry I's grandson, Henry II, to Eleanor of Aquitaine, the scene was set for the Angevins to start to reclaim their old Visigothic Kingdom.

The other momentous event, which occurred after William's death, was the preaching of the 1st crusade in 1089 by Pope Urban II. This had a number of consequences for the "Families." Robert of Normandy decided to go on the crusade and mortgaged his Duchy to his brother William in order to pay for the journey and the outfitting of his followers. Amongst those who accompanied him was Philip de Montgomery, who died on the crusade. The 1st crusade is dealt with in *The God-Kings of Outremer*.

Eustace of Boulogne may have been unsuccessful in his bid to become King of England, but the heirs of Boulogne became Kings of what was at that time regarded as the pre-eminent Christian Kingdom, that of Jerusalem. In a sense, the Conquest of England had been a dress rehearsal for the only really successful crusade, the First Crusade, and it was lead by the heirs of William and his cousins, accompanied by the other major Norman power, the Normans of Southern Italy under the Hautville family.

I mentioned that Henry II's marriage to Eleanor of Aquitaine had formed the basis of an empire stretching from England through Normandy, Maine and far down into southern France, but another inter-family marriage was to bring most of France within their grasp. In 1254 Edward I married Eleanor of Castille. She descended from Jane, Comtesse de Ponthieu – in her own right, the last of the Montgomerys of Ponthieu. Her grandfather, William III of Ponthieu, had married Alice of France and Jane herself married Ferdinand III, King of Castille and Leon. Jane's dowry was her County of Ponthieu and when her great-grand-daughter Eleanor married Edward I, her dowry to Edward was, once again, the County of Ponthieu.[7] Later this was to become the property of another Edward, the Black Prince and Duke of Aquitaine. The so called Hundred Year's War very nearly resulted in one branch of the Ulvungars becoming Kings of England, Scotland, Wales, Ireland, France and Aquitaine. Eventually, they were thwarted by other branches of the same family, who were not prepared to see their English cousins become so powerful... but that is another story. The most unfortunate episode so far as the families were concerned was that during the period from Jane's marriage to the King of Castille and Eleanor's marriage to Edward, the Ponthieu legacy appears to have been suborned by the Catholic Church and Eleanor had the Jews ejected from England.

How have the families of the Conquest survived over the past 1000 years? Some are difficult to trace, and most have had their ups and downs, but many of them have survived and still supply important input into the life of the Nation. I am only going to mention here those families that were directly related to William, and who formed his inner council. They are William's own family of Normandy, the Beaumonts, the Eus (who became Euston or the town of Eu), the FitzOsberns, the Montgomerys and the Boulognes. The Boulognes became Kings of Jerusalem and married into the Royal family of Scotland. I have used *Kelly's Handbook* for 1943 in order to gain a snapshot of the families immediately before the end of the 2nd World War.[8]

The FitzOsbern direct line finished with the death in prison of Roger, the son of William FitzOsbern, but a line that had dropped the "Fitz" became Dukes of Leeds. Then there is the Plantagenet line of the Plantagenet-Hastings, who are Earls of Huntingdon. If you look in Kelly's for 1943 there are a total of 22 Beaumonts listed, including Viscount Allendale. In the same book there are 30 entries for Montgomerie / Montgomery, including the Earl of Eglinton and Winton, and Gen. Sir Bernard Law Montgomery, soon to be Viscount Montgomery of Alamein. Other descendants of Roger de Montgomery took the name Carew and became Baron Carew, also Duke of Brydges and, with yet another name change, the later Lusignan Kings of Jerusalem.

There are undoubtedly a number of other families who can claim descent from the victors of Hastings such as the Grosvenors (Dukes of Westminster), the Courtenays (Earls of Devon), the Bowes-Lyons (Earls of Strathmore), the Devereauxs (Viscount Hereford) and the Harcourts (Viscount Harcourt), but I believe that there are only 32 families who can prove their descent to the satisfaction of genealogists. Perhaps DNA will one day be used to prove or disprove their claims. It is not the function of a study of this sort to decide whether the legacy of the conquest has been good or bad; all that one can say is that these families of Viking (Odonic and Davidic) origin have had an enormous input on Western civilisation in general and Northern Europe in particular.

Many of the families eventually left England and went north to Scotland, where the Catholic Chuch's writ did not run so strongly. Indeed, it was these same families who helped thwart the English conquest of France during the Hundred Years' War. Many still made common cause with their Scandinavian cousins, whose dislike of the Catholic Church was still manifest in the 14th Century. For example, when Henry Sinclair was installed as Jarl of Orkney on 2nd August 1379, he was forbidden by the King of Norway to have anything to do with the Bishop of Orkney without the King's consent. In point of fact, Henry removed the Bishop permanently, though he was never actually accused of the Bishop's murder. There was also an ambitious plan to establish a Northern Commonwealth of Norway, Sweden and Denmark (already united by the treaty of Kalmar), plus Scotland, Orkney, Shetland and the Faroes (united by the bond of Amity signed in 1281), and Iceland, Greenland (part of the Norwegian realm), Markland (Newfoundland), Helluland (Labrador) and Vinland (New England), already settled by descendants of Vikings who looked to Scandinavia as their homeland. This was also to combat the growing power of the Hansa league, which was already referring to the North Sea as the "Oceanus Germanicus" and that of the Roman Church.[9]

I cannot do better than end with a quote from the Toiseach of Clan Sinclair. "If this Northern Commonwealth had materialised the History of the Old and New World would have changed dramatically. Rome would have taken a back seat. **The Odonic Dynasty would have prevailed.**"[10]

References: Chapter 8

1. Ashley, M. (1973) – *The Life and Times of William I*, p. 78, Weidenfield & Nicholson, London, UK.

2. *Ibid.* p. 84 (See also the Anglo-Saxon Chronicle).

3. *Ibid.* p. 84.

4. See Chapter II.

5. Hinde, T. (Editor) (1986) – *The Domesday Book*, p. 11, Hutchinson, London, UK

6. *Peterborough Chronicler* – "All did him homage and became his men and swore him oaths of allegiance."

7. Montgomery, H. *op. cit.* p. 3 & 6.

8. *Kelly's Handbook to the Titled, Landed and Official Classes* (1943), London, UK.

9. Munch, *Norske Folke Historie* 2nd series, Vol.11. p. 95. Also *Diplomaticum. Norvegicum* Vol. 11 pp. 353-355.

10. Letter dated August, 2006.

Chapter IX

All stemmed from this fifth river
All kept the bloodline true
(From Uôuin's River)

The Viking Families and their DNA

When I wrote the first of the books of the *God-Kings* trilogy I pointed out evidence that with the breakup of the Kassite Hegemony in circa 1100 BC, there had been a migration northwards past the Black Sea, which had ended up in Scandinavia at the point when the Nordic countries were just coming out of the Neolithic period and into the Bronze Age. Because the Kassites were already using bronze weapons and travelling by horse drawn transport, the difference in the speed of the migration across Asia Minor and into Scandinavia would have been much quicker than their Paleolithic and Neolithic predecessors; perhaps only a matter of years, rather than the thousand of years previous migrations had taken; witness the Mongols and their horse drawn yurts from a later generation.

At the time of writing *The God-Kings of Europe*, I had no idea of the possibilities of DNA nor knew anything about Haplogroups. It was merely obvious to me that whatever the genetic make-up of the Kassites was, this would become the genetic group of what was to become at least one of if not the dominant ruling class in Scandinavia. I now know that the people of the Fertile Crescent, in and around modern Iraq, were and still are predominantly J and specifically, J2.

Until recently it was believed that the R1b1 Haplotype colonised Europe during the Paleolithic period (circa 25,000 BC), however recent studies have shown that in fact the vast majority of male Y-DNA of the R1b1 haplogroup colonised Europe in the Neolithic period (circa 10,000 BC) with some parts of Europe, in particular Britain, only entering the agricultural revolution as late as 4,000-2,000 BC.[1]

This must also bring into question the colonisation dates for the J2 Haplogroups and in particular, when they moved from the Fertile Crescent into Europe. Did this happen during the Paleolithic or the Neolithic Periods, or even later? Was there more than one such colonisation and why is this important?

There are approximately 110 million males of the R1b1 Haplotype in Europe and it has been clearly shown in the work noted[2] that whilst the female population genetics show little difference from the hunter/gatherer period (Paleolithic or Stone Age) there was a considerable difference in the male DNA, showing that the agricultural revolution brought about by the migration from the Fertile Crescent of the R1b1s, allowed the R1b1 males to mate more successfully with the local females than their hunter/gatherer predecessors. This also means that nearly all surnames groups of European origin will have R1b1 members.

There has been recently considerable work done by the Universities of Leicester, Nottingham and Cambridge led in some cases by Prof. Mark Jobling of the University of Leicester on so-called *Viking* DNA. Actually, the results show that the "Haplogroups R1a, I1a are what most people consider to be reasonably diagnostic of Scandinavian ancestry, when found in Britain." Each of these groups appear to be geographically specific in Scandinavia and therefore their descendants in England in particular will show that their Viking ancestors came from a particular part of Scandinavia.[3]

Indeed, all of the Viking Rulers might have been R1a or I1a, were it not for the Kassite migration, but this migration changed everything, it seems. Let me say that the evidence is statistically small at the moment, but that first results seem compelling.

In Chapter IV, I gave the names of the five people who planned and carried out the Norman Invasion: William of Normandy, Robert de Beaumont, Robert d'Eu, William FitzOsbern and Roger de Montgomery. I furthermore pointed out that they were all cousins, not only from Gunnora and her sisters, but also via the paternal lines as well. One can therefore make the reasonable proposition that they would all show a common ancestor, though of course the common ancestor will vary from each person and their individual relationship. Thus Roger de Montgomery's common ancestor with William of Normandy may not be the same as his with say Robert de Beaumont, and Robert de Beaumont's common ancestor may be different to Roger's and William's.

There are a number of Surname projects including the Winton, Montgomery and Seton projects. The benchmark necessary was to find someone living today who could show well-accepted documentation that they descended from one of the five cousins. There is only one branch of the Montgomerys who have this documented genealogical tree. They are the Montgomerys of Sweden, who were introduced into the Swedish House of Nobles in 1756 with the registration number 1960 B, but with a clear documentation back to 1027 in Normandy.[4] I persuaded one of the males of this family to have a DNA test done. The result, which I have designated M1, is as follows: * (see notes)

DYS #	393	390	19/394	391	385a	385b	426	388	439	389-1	392	389-2	
Allele	12	23	14	10	13	17	11	15	11	13	11	29	
DYS #	458	459a	459b	455	454	447	437	448	449	464a	464b	464c	464d
Allele	14	9	9	11	11	24	15	22	29	13	13	15	16
DYS#	460	H4	YCA IIa	YCA IIb	456	607	576	570	CDY a	CDY b	442	438	
Allele	10	10	19	22	15	15	16	14	34	35	11	9	

This shows immediately that he is J2 Haplotype and is similar to the present day descendants of the Fertile Crescent – though with some differentiation in markers.

There is a further family group who descend from Roger de Montgomery via the 1st Laird of Braidstane, many of whose members went over to Ireland during the Plantation of Ulster and from this group, many emigrated to the USA, New Zealand, Australia and other countries of the New World.

From the Montgomery family project there are at least 18 exact matches with M1 who do not descend from the Swedish Montgomerys. All the descedants of the Swedish House of Nobles are known and registered in their records. Most of the 18 exact matches either have documentation or hearsay evidence that they emigrated from Ireland or the Braidstane and Peebles areas of Scotland. It is therefore reasonable to attribute these to the Braidstane branch.

There is also a well-documented group of Montgomerys who were originally Setons. They descend from the 3rd son of the 1st Earl of Winton, who added Montgomery as a surname so that he could become the 6th Earl of Eglinton and inherit the titles and estates of his uncle, his mother's brother. The problem about this branch of the Setons is that they are not actually Setons, either. They descend from Margaret Seton, who married Alan of Winton in about 1347 (5) and it was from their son, Sir William de Seton, that the Seton-Montgomerys descended, including the present Earl of Eglinton and Winton. Unfortunately, this becomes more and more complicated as Alan de Winton's (or of Winton) surname was not Winton. Winton was a territorial designation. According to *The Seton Family History*, the Wintons were themselves a cadet branch of the Setons. (6) Oh, what a tangled web! However, according to Ian Grimble and backed up by Lyon Court, the later Seton's genealogy from the earlier Setons is suspect (see note 5). What little documentary evidence there is, points to the Setons being descended from Bernard the Dane. I arranged, therefore, for a member of this family who has good documentary evidence of his descent from 6th Earl of Eglinton, who added Montgomery to his Seton surname, to take a DNA test. The results, which I have designated SM1, are as follows: * (see notes)

DYS#	393	390	19/394	391	385a	385b	426	388	439	389/1	392	389/2
Allele	12	23	14	10	13	17	11	15	12	13	11	29

As will immediately be apparent, the results are only 1 off (Marker 439 – underlined) from M1.

According to the charts provided by FTDNA, the time line for a difference of one marker (36/37) is between 19 to 30+ generations. It is important to realise that it is generations and not years. Most genealogists assign 30-35 years for a generation. Now it so happens that SM1's family shows a gap of 44 years per generation for the last 3 generations (dates of birth: Grand father 1816, Father 1868, present 1938) and this is not uncommon for this family. It also happens that we know the exact number of generations between SM1 and the brothers William (dc 985) and Bernard, and that is 34 generations, which makes the average 31 years per generation, well within the accepted norms. It looks, therefore, increasingly likely that the Setons descend as I have long suspected – from William de Montgomery's brother, Bernard the Dane.

However, as I quickly discovered that although the science of DNA is excellent, there is considerable difference of opinion when it comes to interpretation. It appears that the marker 439 mutates somewhat quicker than others, and at least one Montgomery has suggested that the break between M1 and SM1 is about 1320, or thereabouts. This suggests, therefore, that this branch may have intermarried with the line of Bernard the Dane (not an uncommon occurance amongst the Montgomerys or the Setons) and that an ancestor of Alan of Winton may in fact have been a Montgomery. Therefore, since this date came to light I have been looking again at the Seton-Montgomery line.

In c. 1520, Mariot Seton the only daughter of George, 4th Lord Seton, married her 3rd cousin, Hugh 2nd, Earl of Eglinton, by papal dispensation. If they were 3rd cousins, it means that they were five generations away from the Common Male Ancestor. Most genealogists, as I have stated, take a generation to be between 30-35 years, which takes us back to between c. 1340-1370. Margaret Seton married Alan of Winton in c.1347 and it is from them that the line of 4th Lord Seton descends. It was beginning to look as if Alan of Winton, who was supposedly a cadet branch of the Setons, was also in fact a Montgomery, because there are no registered marriages of Montgomery females marrying into this Seton branch, which would be the other possibility.

As I mentioned, there is also some documentary evidence that the Setons descended from Bernard the Dane, brother to William de Montgomery (c. 900), and that their common ancestor was Ragnar Gormsson, or 1st Roger de Montgomery.

According to the manuscript *Bernard le Danois*[7], the families of Beaumont and Harcourt both descend from Bernard the Dane. According to Ms 20780,[8] Bernard the Dane was a brother or uncle of William de Montgomery. One would expect, therefore, that if there was a Harcourt and/or a Beaumont who could trace their descent from Bernard, then they would show a very similar Y-DNA pattern to M1 and possibly identical to SM1. There is only one Harcourt/Horcutt posted on their DNA site but he too, is J2 (J2b1).

There are of course a considerable number of Montgomerys who are not J2. This is because, although under Clan Law, with all members of the Clan assumed to be descended from an eponymous, the reality is that the Chiefly family members are often of a totally different male descent to the members of the Clan – particularly in Scotland, where a female can become Chief of a Clan and her son or daughter inherits, thus making the male DNA lineage totally different, as witness the present Chief of the Hays, whose father was Moncrieffe of that Ilk. Furthermore, in Scotland surnames are of recent usage and in many cases only came into being after the 1745 rebellion, when certain Clans were proscribed and people who lived in a particular district took the names of their local Lord in order to have a legal protector or indeed, the necessity of a surname in certain legal documents.

In fact, my own great-grand-uncle, in order to have a larger entourage than the local Cunningham, with whom they were in dispute, went down to the local pub and offered 2 shillings and 6 pence and a pint of whisky to anyone who would take the name Montgomery. This was not uncommon. In fact, I suspect that some people took the money from both the Montgomerys and Cunninghams and changed their surnames according to who was paying them at the time. They would have had absolutely no connection by blood with the Chief concerned.

In England too, immediately after the Norman Conquest, there were no surnames but people were often said to be "of" somewhere. An example of this was in the territories of Roger de Montgomery, 1st Earl of Shrewsbury. He conquered large parts of north Wales and founded the town and county of Montgomery, now Powys. The landholders of his territories would have been "of Montgomery" and over the years, as the custom changed, so the "of" was dropped and they simply became Montgomery. Although some may have been the result of liaisons between the ruling lord and local women, the vast majority would have simply been from whatever haplogroup was in ascendancy in the local area and, given the general preponderance of R1b1 in Europe, a great many would have been from this group.

We know, for example, that some Montgomerys descend from a man-at-arms called Picot, who held Clun under Roger de Montgomery.[9] His descendants adopted the name Montgomery when Robert de Bellême was dispossessed by Henry I.

In America, after the emancipation of the slaves, many ex-slaves adopted the surname of their previous owners, so I would expect there to be a number of Americans who descend from the Montgomery plantation ex-slaves and who have the surname Montgomery. Having said that, it is very possible that many are actually Montgomerys on the male side, as liaisons between the owners and their female slaves were quite common.[10]

Furthermore, in parts of Scotland the habit of Highland Hospitality, whereby an important visitor was offered the daughter of the house as a bedmate during his stay, often caused the genetics of a father to be entirely different from the family name. In Ayrshire in the 1700s the percentage of illegitimate births rose to nearly 20% of the population. There is a gentleman who is only 1 allele off from SM1, but with a totally different name and no known connection to the Montgomerys, but who almost certainly descends from a Montgomery. His Y-DNA, which I have labelled MB1, is as follows: *

393	390	19-394	391	385a	385b	426	388	439	389-1	392	389-2
12	23	14	10	13	17	11	15	11	13	11	29

Identical to M1 and 1 off SM1

The Setons too, have a number of different groupings. Besides the MS1 that I have mentioned, there are other Setons who are J2 but show up to 14 different allele numbers from both M1 and MS1. These are probably the original Setons, if I can call them that; descended from the Sire de Seton who held the town of Sai, near to Exmes in Lower Normandy, of which the Montgomerys were made Counts in about 911. It is probable, therefore, that they held from the Montgomery Counts of Exmes and were part of the Viking group who settled in Lower Normandy with Ragnar Gormsson (see Chapter I) and presumably were related to him. These Setons came over with William the Conqueror in 1066 and settled in and around the Northampton area, though there has also been a suggestion that they were related to the family of Lens from Boulogne.[11]

But to prove my point I needed DNA from a descendant of William the Conqueror, the Eu and FitzOsbern families. The Eus had petered out in the 1150s and I believe that the FitzOsberns had been wiped out. It was unlikely that I was going to be able to persuade the authorities to exhume the bodies of William the Conqueror or any of his sons but there was a family, amongst the highest of British aristocracy, who claimed, albeit without any documentation, to descend from an illegitimate son of Duke Richard II. I had to agree to total anonymity and that the test could only be carried out in a trial where his DNA could not be specifically linked in. He too, tested J2. Unfortunately, without documentation this proves nothing, but it was indicative that many of the Viking families surrounding William himself and his cousins were J2. It looked as if the House of Brocus was indeed Kassite.[12]

However, quite out of the blue I was informed by an e-mail contact that a gentleman on one of the DNA sites, who descends from the nephew of William FitzOsbern, and who held the manor of Wendle, had had his DNA tested, which he expected to be I1 and could not understand why he had come out as J2, which he assumed to be Jewish. At the moment of publication I have been unable to contact this gentleman directly, but if true, then as William FitzOsbern was a first cousin to William I, it would seem, with the other DNA tests to be proof, that the Ducal/Royal Family of the Normans and their cousins were J2.

There was one more intriguing bit of information. The Fairbairn/Fairburn family name project show mostly I1, with of course the inevitable R1b, but there was one gentleman who showed not just J2, but identical to M1. Now, I do not know the history of the Fairbairns but clearly they were Scandinavian in origin and I wondered if they had, in the past, been associated with Harald Fairhair (King of Norway –d. 933). Could they all have been his warband, originally taking the name "son of Fairhair," which became Fairbairn (bairn means youngster in Scots)? Was the only J2 a direct descendant of Harald Fairhair? As both the 1st Roger de Montgomery and Harald Fairhair descended from Herioldus Brocus, it would make sense. Or perhaps all matches to M1 descend from Roger de Montgomery. This is, of course, pure speculation but I thought intriguing. There are also Montgomery I1s, which I assume would have had a similar origin as part of the Viking Warbands attached to one or other of the Viking leaders. They would have married into the family and have eventually taken the name of their leader's family's main title (eg. de Montgomery or de Beaumont, etc.).

From all of this information it seems likely that the R1b1s came over during the Neolithic period and replaced the resident males and became the farmers of Europe.

One would expect, therefore, that all family surnames of European stock would have a considerable number of R1b1 amongst their members. The question that then must be asked is, when did the J2s, who became the leaders, arrive in Europe? There is more than one possibility.

They could have arrived during the Paleolithic period, remained there during the R1b1 invasion and then become the warrior caste based on their hunter-gatherer skills. The problem with this theory is that they would have had little chance of continuing their genes under the prevailing R1b1 culture, particularly as the R1b1s had superior stone tools and presumably superior stone weapons.

It is more likely that they arrived afterwards, during the Bronze Age or early Iron Age, with superior wearonry but still needing to be fed. It seems likely, therefore, that they agreed to the farmers continuing to farm, but that the farmers now had to provide a percentage of their crops to this upper class in return for "protection," even if it was only protection from the upper class itself. Protection rackets go back a long way – witness the Mongols. But if they were J2s then they must have come from Mesopotamia, where the greatest number of these haplotypes existed and indeed still exist today. I would therefore suggest that these were the Kassites of Babylon, (13) who we know migrated from the Fertile Triangle about 1,000 BC. (14) This was my premise at the beginning of book 1 of this trilogy, *The God-Kings of Europe*, and it seems that this premise was correct. Many of the R1b1 were effectively reduced to peasantry; indeed, this would almost certainly be why they became and still are the largest group of male genes in Europe.

To summarise: The Winton/Seton/Montgomerys may well not have descended from the original Setons, but from a Montgomery cadet branch and the five cousins William of Normandy, Robert d'Eu, Robert de Beaumont, William FitzOsbern and Roger de Montgomery were probably all J2,[15] as were many of the families surrounding them and with whom they intermarried. The evidence is small but compulsive. Further DNA testing will be required to prove or disprove this.

References Chapter 9

1. Balaresque, P. et al (2010) – *A Predominantly Neolithic Origin for European Paternal Lineages*, Article 10.1371, Plos Biology Journal, Dept. of Genetics, University of Leicester, Lab. D'Etude du Polymorphisme de l'AND, Faculté de Médecine, Nantes and others.

2. Ibid.

3. Bowden et al (2008) – *Excavating past population structures by surname based sampling. The genetic legacy of Vikings in northwest England*, Journal of Molecular Biology Evolution, Feb. 25 (2) p. 301-9. Also, e-mail to the author dated 16th March 2010.

4. *Sveriges Adels-Kalender* (1995), p. 396, Montgomery.

5. Grimble, I. (1984 edition) – *Scottish Clans & Tartans*, p.245, Hamlyn, London.

6. http://www2.thesetonfamily.com:8080/directory/family_of_winton.htm.

7. See references Chapter 1, note 16.

8. Ibid, note 6.

9. *The Domesday Book*, Shropshire Gazetteer, p 225, Hutchinson, London.

10. Foster E. A. et al (1998) – *Jefferson fathered slave's last child*, Nature 396: 27-28.

11. Platts, B. (1985) – *Scottish Hazard* Vol. 1, p. 172, Procter Press, London.

12. For the House of Brocus see: Montgomery, H. (2006) – *The God-Kings of Europe*, p. 84, The Book Tree, San Diego, CA, USA.

13. Montgomery, H. (2008) – *The God-Kings of Outremer*, App. S, p. 164, The Book

Tree, San Diego, CA, USA.

14. Montgomery, H. (2006) – *The God-Kings of Europe*, Chapter 1, The Book Tree,

San Diego, CA, USA.

15. Jobling M.A. (2001) – *In the name of the father*, Journal of Trends in Genetics 16: 356-362.

* All DNA results were done by Family Tree DNA, and all the persons so tested have given me permission to use their results. In the case of the Fairbairns, this is in the public domain. All three have been done to 37 markers but for the purpose of this chapter I have only shown SM1 & MB1 to 12 markers because they are otherwise identical.

APPENDIX I

1a. Polygamy

In this book I have noted in passing the matter of polygamy. It is a subject that most historians either ignore or scout around. I think, however, it is time to bring this matter into the open. Most historians accept that the Merovingians and the early Carolingians were polygamous and particularly that Charlemagne had several wives and concubines concurrently. The Church in the 9th and 10th centuries tried to pretend that this did not happen and called one or other of the wives mistresses. This, however, disguised a reality. The Frankish and Norse noble families were by nature, tradition and inclination polygamous. If you look at the Genealogies I-IV you will see immediately that this continued until late in the 10th and into the beginning of the 11th century.

Harold Bluetooth had at least two wives concurrently.

Sweyn Forkbeard married Sigrid before the death of Gunnhild.

Richard I of Normandy was married to both Emma and Gunnora at the same time, even though the Church tried to pretend that only Emma was his wife. If this had been so, then why did nobody raise the question of the legitimacy of Richard, Robert and his other children?

Rollo was married to both Poppa and Gizelle at one and the same time. Again, the priests would have us believe that Poppa was a mistress and again, why did nobody raise the question of William "Longsword's" legitimacy?

William "Longsword" himself had two wives concurrently, Espriota and Leutgarda.

In fact, there is even a case for making Herleve a second wife to Robert rather than the mistress that everyone proclaims. My only comment is that by now the Church was becoming too powerful for the Normans to continue their customary behaviour.

It is noticeable, however, that neither Cnut, who was married to both Aelgifa of Northampton and Emma of Normandy at the same time, nor Harald Hardrada, who was also married to two wives at one and the same time, thought that the Church's censure was important. The Catholic Church was much less powerful in Scandinavia.

107

1b. The Religious Beliefs

There is a case to be made that neither the Merovignians nor the early Carolignians were Christian in the accepted sense. It could be argued that they were pagan or possibly even Jewish. The point that Prof. Zuckerman makes is perfectly valid. If the Church was fulminating against Charlemagne's most senior nobles converting to Judaism, and Charlemagne was supporting the nobles concerned, then it brings into doubt Charlemagne's own beliefs, especially as he had married a Jewish princess. (See Zuckerman, A.J. (1972) – *A Jewish Princedom in Feudal France 768-900*, Columbia University Press, New York & London, Chap. 4.) In traditional Judaism, one could have more than one wife!

1c. The Position of Jews in England Under the Norman and Angevin Kings

It has already been shown that the Carolingian Emperors of the 9th Century had taken the Jews under their special protection (see Bartlett, R. op. cit. p. 351). The Norman Kings made the position even more clear by granting them a series of Charters, one of which, issued in 1201, says that they were permitted to reside in the King's lands, to travel where they would and to have secure possession of their "lands, fiefs, pledges and escheats" (reverted estates). In Law, a Jew need only appear before the Royal Judges. In a case between Christian and Jew, the Plaintiff, whether Jew or Christian, had to have witnesses of both religions. In the absence of witnesses, a Jew could clear himself by an oath on the roll of the Law. Very importantly, where a Christian brought a case against a Jew, unless it was the Crown, it was "to be judged by the Jews fellows." The only other group with similar rights were the members of the Peerage.

Furthermore, their rights in chattels and debts were guaranteed and they were free from tolls and customs. In return, the Jews created wealth for the King by trade and money lending and were taxed separately to the rest of the populace.

There is a photograph of a Jewish ritual bath recently uncovered by archaeologists in what was Milk Street in the old city of London and close to the White Tower, built by William to guard London. This bath was built shortly after the conquest.

The other interesting point is that Catharism appears to have started in the Narbonne Area and somewhere between 800-1100 gradually moved north to encompass Beziers, Montsegur, Montreal, Toulouse, Lavaur, Montaubon, Cahors, Niort and Thuors. (see Barber, M. (2000) – *The Cathars*, Pearson

Educational Ltd., Essex, UK, pp. 260-266.) I have shown in *The God-Kings of Europe* how early Judaic-Christianity gradually became Elchasaic and eventually, Catharism.

1d. The St. Clairs and Sinclairs

The information regarding the adoption of the name St. Clair and later Sinclair is based upon documents in their possession and kindly provided by Major Niven Sinclair.

1e. The Aristocracy and Titles

There seems to be considerable difference of opinion as to who constituted the Aristocracy and what titles they used. The Law recognised only the law for the "Free" and there was no difference between them unless they were Jews (see above). Therefore, there was no unified group of people at the point of the Conquest who could be called "Nobles" with special privileges (see Bartlett, R. *op. cit.* p. 207). You might be called Earl or Knight – the Law made no differentiation – only the King was above the Law. There were indeed words used in Latin documents such as "Nobilis," "Generosus," "Potens" and "Magnus," but whether these indicated that a particular group of people were so called must, I think, be said to be non-proven. The highest title in Anglo-Saxon times was undoubtedly Earl, which is of Anglo-Scandinavian origin and which was generally rendered in Latin as "Comes." Again, Bartlett suggests that there were only 7 of these titles at the time of and shortly after the conquest, namely Huntingdon/Northampton, Kent, Northumberland, Chester, Shrewsbury and East Anglia. I am not so convinced. It seems to me that we are talking here of the most senior of these Earls or, if you wish, what I have termed "Earls Palatine." Indeed, according to William of Malmesbury, William Rufus, in talking to Roger de Montgomery at the time of the 1088 rebellion, actually calls them "Duces" or Dukes (see W. Malm., Gesta Regum 4.306). It seems to me more likely that anyone with 100 Knights' fees would have been classified as an Earl. There is also the question of what a great Count from the continent who happened to have English land would be called in documents. If he were called in Latin "Comes Arundelensis," was he Earl of Arundel?

Whilst as I accept that there were only seven "Great Earldoms" or "Earls Palatine," I am not so sure about the titles used by other Barons and magnates.

Appendix II

Notes on Genealogies

Author's note: The information in this appendix was based upon the researches of the late Dr. B. G. Montgomery (Stockholm & Oxford). Much of this has been previously published by him in *Ancient Migrations and Royal Houses* (1968). I am most grateful to my distant cousin in Sweden, Sophie Montgomery, for facilitating the notes and the published and un-published work of her father. The conclusions in this appendix are, however, mine and do not necessarily reflect the late B. G. Montgomery's point of view.

****

According to the *Annals of Fulda*, Godfrid (Snorre's Gudröd Vejdekong) was the brother of king Horic (*Horic Regem Danorum & Gudurm fratris ejus*), but the *Three Fragments* tell us that Godfrid was the son of Ragnaill and the father of king Ingvar. This must be correct since otherwise, Godfrid would have had a son with the same name. At that time father and son never shared the same name, unless the son was born after the father's death. Godfrid was chief of Fingall and of the Isles in 835.

The *Fragments* contain the following interesting passage:

"Amhlaeibh went from Erin to Lochlann to wage war on the Lochlanns, and to aid his father Godfridh, for the Lochlanns had made war against him, his father having come for him; but it would be tedious to relate the cause of the war, and besides it appertains but little to us, though we have knowledge of it, for our business is not to write whatever may belong to Erin, nor even all these; for the Irish suffer evils, not only from the Lochlanns, but they also suffer injuries from one another."

If the author of these lines had known that they would be carefully studied more than a thousand years after they were written and that the cause of the war between Godfrid and the Lochlanns would become a matter of intense interest to historians of the present generation he would, no doubt, have given us the details which he found so tedious to relate. We must be grateful, however, for the information he *has* given us. The war mentioned took place in 872 when the military forces of Denmark were heavily engaged in England

and Scotland. Since Amhlaeibh (Olaf) went to Lochlann to aid his father against Lochlanns we may reasonably assume from these sources:

1. Neither Godfrid nor Olaf considered themselves as Lochlanns,

2. Godfrid had left the Hebrides and settled in Norway,

3. He was the Danish King of Westfold and South Jutland.

A Danish king in Westfold would become an easy prey to bellicose native petty kings in that part of Norway if they united against him at a moment when he could expect no immediate reinforcements from Denmark. But this was probably not the cause of the war referred to in the Irish document. We must think again. The father of Harald Fair Hair, king of Norway, was Halfdan the Black. He has wrongly been ranked among petty kings by Snorre and others who have produced fantastic pedigrees for this king, tracing his descent from the ancient kings of Upsala. These pedigrees are supported by no evidence. On the other hand, there is plenty of evidence to show that Halfdan the Black was the son of Ragnvald Heiôumhaerri, king of Westfold, son of Godfrid, king of Denmark, son of Herioldus Brochus.

Halfdan's victory of Hafrsfjord over his brother Godfrid and his nephew Olaf (Ingvar's brother, see Appendix III) brought Westfold and other parts of South Norway under his dominion. This battle took place in 872 and Halfdan's son Harald (Fair Hair) was too young at the time to accompany his father on that campaign.

The story of Harald's proposal to Princess Ragnhild of Denmark, the daughter of the younger king Horic, is for many reasons absurd. In all probability *she* was his mother, since tradition is unanimous to the effect that the name of Halfdan's spouse was Ragnhild. This would also be in keeping with the fact that the petty kings of Norway so readily submitted to the ruling of the young king after Halfdan's death in 877.

Harald's sons Eric, surnamed Blodyx, was sometime king of Norway and later on, of Northumberland (once ruled by his grandfather Halfdan), and Hakon succeded his brother as king of Norway.

It seems reasonable to assume that Horic and Raghnaill's brother Olaf is identical with the king Olaf, who resided at Birka on the arrival of St. Anscharius about 850. As far as we know, there is no other king who bore that name at that time except Amhlaeibh (Olaf) Conung, the son of the king of Lochlann, who invaded Ireland in 852. The elder king Horic of Denmark, whose brother's name was Olaf, sent a letter of introduction for Anscharious to king Olaf of Birka in order to facilitate his mission. Rimbert tells us that Olaf invaded Courland. This country had a population related to the Achaians of West Scania and two of its' towns, Seeburgh and Apulia, are mentioned by Rimbert. The land where Libau and Memel now stands was at that time under water and Seeburgh must have been situated on the coastline. Apulia is the correct Latin translation of Puglie, which in Achaian would have been Fuglie or Fiaeliae. In this case, Apulia must be identified with the town Siaulisi in Lithuania, situated about seven miles east of Memel.

Olaf had two sons, one being Horic, king of Denmark and father of Ragnhild, who married Halfdan the Black; and the other, Anund, king of Birka before 844 ("Ermunder Kunung Olafs sun" – *Series Runica Prima,* from Danish State Archives).

Godfrid, King of Westfold, had two sons who became kings of Dublin, one after the other. In the Irish annals they were known as Amhlaeibh and Imhar, but the Saxon chronicles call them Hinguar & Ubba. In Scandinavian sagas and chronicles they are designated as "bastard sons of Ragnar Lodbrok," which is nonsense. In 871 they raided Scotland and plundered the country. Their fleet on this occasion numbered 200 ships (*Three Fragments*). The same event is recorded in the *Annals of Ulster.* Mathew of Westminster has the year at 870. Ingvar died in *Christo 873* (*Annals of Ulster*), and Olaf lost his life in a struggle with king Alfred's men in Devonshire 878. It was on this occasion that he flew the banner of the Raven, embroidered by his sisters. Ingvar had two sons, Godfrey, his heir, and Sitric, who murdered his brother in 884 and succeeded him in 885.

It is perhaps as well to note here that the Danish name *Oluf* simply means *O'Ulf* (*Mac d'Uff*) i.e. descendant of Ulf. (They are therefore proclaiming that they are descended from Ata-Ulf [The ancestor-Ulf], who married Maria of the Elchasaites, as detailed in *The God Kings of Europe*, Chap. 1). Godfrid, Gudrod or Goder, the eldest son of Herioldus Brochus, alias Hylthetan, was king of most of Denmark. He was killed while preparing a great expedition against Charlemagne in 810. In the fighting that ensued between the rival claimants to the Crown, Godfrid's sons Horic and Olaf killed Anulo, Halfdan's eldest son. "Olaf Kunung Rings bane, Goder son," says *Series Runica Prima.* Anulo's younger brother Harald (Herioldus) and Ragnar (Ragbinfridus) then turned to the Emperor for support and eventually recovered the lands conquered by Godfrid's sons. According to Adam of Bremen, discord later arose between Harald and Ragnar and the latter was compelled to leave the country.

Harald, king of South Jutland and Lethra, and his son Godfrid, were baptized at Mayence in 826. Harald received the land of the Frisians between the mouths of the Scheldt and the Ems as a fief under the Emperor. This Christian king of Denmark did not remain in power for very long. He eventually settled in his Frisian country and later in Gaul, but was murdered there in 852. His son Godfrid entered the Seine with a fleet in 850 and after his father's death, he was granted a fief in Neustrie by Charles-le-Chauve.

Cornelius Hamsfort (1546-1627) who was the owner of a most important collection of ancient documents and chronicles relating to Danish history (Regum Danorum series) states that Ragnar succeeded his brother Harold as King of the Cimbri of Seeland. If this is true, and I see no reason to doubt it, then Ragnar was no doubt Overlord of the Cimbric population in central Jutland, the Danish isles and the south of Sweden.

The *Three Fragments* contain the following:

"At this time (869) the Aunites, i.e. the Danes, came with countless forces to Caer Ebroic (York), and destroyed the city, which they took, and this was the beginning of great troubles and difficulties to the Britons. For not long before this time every kind of war and commotion prevailed in Lochlann, which arose from this cause; i.e. the two younger sons of Albdan, King of Lochlann, expelled the eldest son Raghnall, son of Albdan, because they feared he would seize the kingdom of Lochlann after their father (had he been the eldest son he would have been the lawful heir); and Raghnall came with his three sons to Innsi Orc, and Raghnall tarried there with his youngest son. But his elder sons, with a great host, which they collected from every quarter, came on to the British Isles, being elated with pride and ambition to attack the Franks and Saxons. They thought that their father had returned to Lochlann immediately after setting out, but now their pride and youthful ambition induced them to row forward across the Cantabrian sea, (the sea which is between Erin and Spain), until they reached Spain, and they were guilty of many outrages in Spain, both killing and plundering. They afterwards crossed the Gaditanean Straits, where the Mediterranean Sea goes into the Atlantic Ocean, and arrived in Africa; where they fought a battle with the Mauretani, in which a great slaughter of the Mauretani was made."

It would seem that Raghnall (Ragnar) had under him not only the Cimbres of Seeland, mentioned by Hamsfort, but also the Chattic Aunites i.e. the Visigoths of Ragnarici, Westrogothia and Ostrogothia. Birka and Håtuna were northern outposts of his maritime and commercial empire along the east coast of Sweden.

The events in the Fragments seem to have taken place some time between the years 844-859 (*Annales Bertiniani*). Scottish Chronicles, in Innes, make the following reference to an invasion of Scotland in the reign of Kenneth Mac Alpin (843-58): "The Danish pirates, wasting Pictavia, advanced into the interior, as far as Clunie, in Stormont, and Dunkeld on the Tay, under the influences of Ragnar Lodbrog, whose desire was plunder, and whose delight was blood. He soon afterwards met his merited fate in Northumberland, amid a congenerous people."

The raids on Spain and Morocco were no doubt carried out in conjunction with the contemporary invasions of Gaul. In both cases Raghnall's elder sons

Sigfrid (Frotho), in *Series Runica Prima* called "Siwarth Kunung sun Regners Lodbrogh," and Bjorn Ironside, styled "Biorn Kunung Jarnsithe," were the leaders of the operations. In the Frank annals, Bjorn is called "Bier Costae Ferrae, Lothbroci Regis filius," which indicates his descent from Herioldus Brochus. The word *filius* is used, as his father Ragnar would have been known as Ragnar "Lothbrok," being of the House of Brochus (see Ulvungar Dynasty Genealogy II). Equally the word *filius* may be construed as "descendant," as it is sometimes used in other documents.

Sigfrid, called Frotha in the *Annals of Clonmacnois*, makes his first appearance in history during the Danish occupation of Ireland, in the company of his brother Awuslir (a distortion of Burislav – see following). He left Ireland but returned with his brother Ivar (Bagsaeg) in 852 (*Annals of Innisfallen*). Ivar occupied Limerick and Frotho, and established himself at Waterford. His name in the annals was at that time Sitric. He seems to have left Ireland, as we find him later in the same year moving up the Seine to join the forces of his brother Bjorn. The following winter was passed in a camp, but in the spring he took his forces to the Loire. He was wounded during the siege of Nantes that summer. In 855 he sailed up the Seine and penetrated as far as Perche in Champagne (*Chron. Fontaneille*, in Perche). His name in the Frank annals is Sidroc.

After these events, Frotho seems to have retired to Denmark. He did not take an active part in the conquest of East-Anglia and Northumberland. The leaders of these operations were his brother Ivar Bagsaeg and his son Gorm (Guthrum). Frotho was too old and may also have suffered from his wound. Yet the chronicles have given him the cognomen "Victor Anglia's" since he was the king of Denmark under whose auspices the conquest was successfully carried out. He is also called "Anglicus I" and his son, who was the actual conqueror, is known as "Anglicus II," in Danish, "hin Enske." Frotho's brother Ivar was killed at the battle of Ashdown (Assandune) in 871.

After the sanguinary battle of Saultcourt in 881 when the combined forces of the Vikings in Gaul had been thoroughly routed by Louis of France, the peoples of Western Europe were hoping for a long breathing space; but already in November of that year a new army of invaders moved up the Meuse and took up winter quarters at Haslou. The commanders of this force were Sigfrid and Godfrid, both styled kings in the chronicles. Sigfrid was the son of Hemming, King of Denmark ("Siwarth Hemminag sun," *Series Runica Prima*) and Godfrid was his nephew, the son of Harald, King of South Jutland, whom some chroniclers have mistaken for Helge, the father of Gorm Grandaevus. Sigfrid had with him his son Gorm (Wurm) and his brother Halfdan* (contracted Hals or Half, short for Halfdanus), both designated princes (see note below and Appendix IV). They moved up the Meuse and took up winter-quarters in a fortified camp at Eslo, not far from Maastricht.

The following summer this army seized and ravaged the towns of Maastrich, Liege, Coblenz, Cologne and Bonn and the surrounding country; in Aachen they turned the Imperial palace into a stable for their horses, while other imperial castles such as Zilpich, Jülich and Nuys were burnt to the ground, as were the rich monasteries of Pruym, Stablo and Malmedy. After this display of barbaric warfare in the heart of the Emperor's domain, the Viking army returned to their camp at Eslo. Emperor Charles-le-Gras raised a large army to destroy these invaders and their camp was besieged. Yet Sigrid and Godfrid won the battle – not by superior courage and military experience, but as a result of a very simple ruse and the lavish use of bribes. An agreement was eventually signed according to which the invaders were bought off by treasure in gold and silver to the amount of more than two thousand pounds, which was a huge sum in those days, against a pledge to abandon imperial territory and not return. Both kings agreed to be baptized. Godfrid obtained all Friezeland, including the fief previously held by king Harald and his son Godfrid, from the mouth of the Weser in the north to the mouth of the Scheldt in the south. Not on this occasion, as some chronicles state, but on another, the Emperor bestowed upon him in marriage Gisella, daughter of the late king Lothair of Lorraine, and his first cousin. All this seems incredible, yet more natural if we keep in mind that the Lodebrochi claimed descent from Hlodio and Ataulf, the rulers of Friezeland earlier, when Gaul was a Roman province.

Godfrid did not long enjoy his exalted position. In 885 he fell into a trap cleverly set by the Emperor himself, the Bishop of Cologne, and the Counts Henry of Saxon-Thüringen and Everard of Friuli, whose interests he had grievously injured. He arrived in the company of his wife, unarmed and with insufficient escort for a conference with the three last mentioned gentlemen. After a short dispute and an angry retort by Godfrid, he was cut down by Count Everard and killed. So were his men. The Bishop withdrew. He had persuaded Queen Gisella to quit her husband before this murder took place.

After the murder of Godfrid, Sigfrid became the leader of all the Viking operations in France, including the besieging of Paris in 885. He returned to Friesland the same year, but was killed in 887. The Danish kings Gorm (alias Guthrum) and Gorm (alias Gormeric and Gorm-hin-rikhe) have often been mistaken for each other and on the following grounds. They were both styled kings in Denmark, they had the same first name and they were both the sons of kings with the first name Sigfrid (alias Frotho). In fact, they were second cousins and ruled over different parts of England.

The elder Frotho, who was a cousin of the younger king with the same name, was one of the leaders of the great Danish expedition to Ireland in 833. His son Guthrum, whose Christian name was Athelstan, conquered East Anglia, but apparently he gave his father the honour of this conquest. Thus *Series*

Runica Prima says "Frotho kunung han van Engeland, Gorm kunung Anske." (Frotho rex qui Angliam vicit, Gormo Anglicus rex.) Guthrum was defeated by King Alfred in 878 but was allowed to remain in England on condition that he became a Christian. According to some authorities he died in 890, while others say 891. The younger Frotho, surnamed the Frisian (In Danish records, "hin Frikhe," a contraction of Frisian. Some authors have translated this into Latin as "Vegetus," which is incorrect), son of Hemming, son of Halfdan, son of Herioldus, was the father of Gormeric, prince of Denmark and later King of Northumberland, with the Christian name Guthred. He was also called "hin-rikhe," which means "the rich." The annals of St. Bertin mention that Sigfrid and Gorm in 882 extorted a *Danageld* of several thousand pounds of silver and gold. His share in this indemnity seems to offer a plausible explanation of his cognomen. After Sigfrid's death in 887, Gorm was elected King of Northumberland, but was killed in a battle with Godfrey, King of Dublin, in 894.

An old French manuscript in the Bibliotheque Nationale (Ms francais 20780, earlier quoted Généalogie d'Allemagne, Cabinet des tires 20. 780, fols. 221-23), belonging to the collection of Mézeray, contains the following passage:

> "Roger Gommer I du nom fit bastir la ma (aison) nomma de son surnom et de la situation du lieu qui lui escheut au département de Normandie. Il fut le premier comte de Montgomery et l'un des princes qui accompagnerent le Duc Roul a la conqueste de Neustrie environ l'an 885 (should be 895), du quel vindret Guillaume I premier du nom, et Bernard surnommé le Danois qui fut gouverneur du jeune Duc Richard et lequel par sa grande prudence et sagesse sauva la vie et l'Estat dudit Richard."

> Translation: "Roger Gommer I the first of his house and name and his surname is situated in a department of Normandie. He was the first count de Montgomery and one of the princes (Danish?) who accompanied Duke Rollo on his conquest of Neustria in 885 (should be 895). From him descends William 1st (of Montgomery) first of his name, and Bernard surnamed the Dane who was governor to the young Duke Richard and who by his great prudence and wisdom saved the life and estate of the said Richard."

Le Marquis du Four de La Londe wrote in a letter (28th Jan. 1948) on the subject of this manuscript: "Its provenance is interesting, because Mézeray was a Norman, from the same parts where the Montgomery were known and had their estates. United through the bonds of family and friendship with all the nobles and all the great men in the vicinity of Argentan, he had a better opportunity than anybody else of informing himself about their genealogies and to get access to their archives. Moreover, he was a learned man and a first rate researcher. Eudes de Mézeray (1611-83) was the historiographer of Louis XIV and the permanent secretary of the French Academy."

The only Danish prince with the name of Gorm, who took part in the battles of Neustrie in 885, was the son of Sigfrid the Frisian. After the death of Gorm (Gormeric, Guthred) in 894 his eldest son Ragnar (in French, Roger) returned to Neustrie. According to the Nordic custom he used his father's name, plus the ending son as a cognomen (Ragnar Gormsson – In French Roger Go(r)merici). He was also called Roger Magnus in 911 when he, now a Christian count, restored the devastated convent of Sancta Opportuna (Cartullary in Bibl. Nat) in the proximity of Saint Germain de Montgomery. He is no doubt identical with Count Roger who played such an important part in the negotiations between Louis d'Outremer and William Longsword of Normandy, one of his most intimate friends. He died in Normandy soon afterwards, in 912. (See *Montgomery Millennium* p. 1, but some have confused him with his son, also Roger – see also Richerii Historarium II, ch. 28.) His grandson William, who bore the same Christian name as the Duke, was the grandfather of Count Hugh and great grandfather of Count Roger, who was second-in-command to William the Conqueror.

Among Rollo's nearest relations were his uncle Helgi and his cousin Gorm Grandaevus, both kings of Denmark. *Series Runica Prima* makes "Gorm Kunung hin Gamle" the son of "Hartald Kunung Biorns sun." Yet we know from the Irish annals that the sons of Gorm the Old were called Mac Elchi (or Elgi), and Gorm himself is referred to as "Tomar Mac Elchi" i.e. Gorm, the son of Helge. Moreover, the same annals record his two sons, Canute, who was killed in Ireland 936, and Harald, surnamed Bluetooth, well known to history.

The name of Gorm's father, therefore, was Helgi. Adam of Bremen, who was in direct communication with the Danish king Sven Estridsson (1047-76), further affirms this conclusion by the statement that Helge or Heilligo from Northmannia was King of Denmark after the battle of Louvain in 891, where the flower of the Danish nobility perished. Since Bjorn Ironside is recorded as the grandfather of Gorm Grandaevus and Helge as his father, Helge must be the son of Bjorn. Rollo's uncle Helge (Helcius) is mentioned by William of Jumieges in an interpolation quoted by Ordericus Vitalis, with reference to Roger de Toni (Teny, Toeni). In the Benedictine version of this manuscript he is said to "belong to the lineage of the wicked Hulcius" (de stripe mala Hulcius). Helge was the paternal uncle of Rollo and his companion in arms during the conquest of Normandy. This reading is undoubtedly correct; but Dudo calls him Malahulcius, i.e. Helge with the divided chin, though I suspect this is merely a poor medieval Latin pun.

Note: (*According to the *Annals of Fulda*, Sigfrid and his brother Halfdan had a conference with Louis the German at Ejderen in 873 and presented him with a golden hilted sword.)

Appendix III

Rollo's Names

There is some dispute as to Rollo's ancestry and nationality at the time of his invasion of Normandy. Recently historians including David Crouch and myself have come to the conclusion that Richer of Rheims was right to call Rollo's father Keitel. However, whilst Prof. Crouch leaves the matter there, I have, with the help of my distant cousin, the late Dr. B. G. Montgomery, been able to piece together a genealogy.

Snorre Sturluson, who wrote his saga of the Scandinavian kings at the beginning of the 13th century, makes Rollo the son of the Norwegian Earl Rognvald of More. Many arguments have been raised for and against this unproven statement. As a rule, the Norwegian historians have supported Snorre, while the Danes have relied on the much earlier chronicles of France, Britain, Germany and Denmark, and claim him for their own country. There is no doubt that in this discussion, patriotic feelings have sometimes obscured the conclusions drawn by the contending parties; but such feelings are particularly out of place in this connection, since Rollo, strictly speaking, was neither a Norwegian nor a Dane, but an Orkney man, a Hunedane, and a native of Moere in Sweden, though the son of a Danish king. (There is some disagreement amongst scholars, but this is the opinion of B. G. Montgomery and myself.)

Some Historians of other countries have also sided against Snorre. The literature on this controversial subject includes the following books and essays:

J. Lair, *Introductory Notes to Dudon de Saint-Quentin, Mémoires de la Société des Angtiquitaires de Normandie*, 1885.

J. Worsac, *Den danske Erobring af England og Normanniet*, 1863.

J. Steenstrup, *Normannerne*, 1873-82.

E. Wahlberg, Sur l'Origine de Rollon, 1913.

J. Revel, *Historie des Normans*, 1918.

B. G. Montgomery, *Ancient Migrations and Royal Houses*, 1968.

In *Rollo och Gange Rolf*, Historisk Tidskrift för Skåneland, 1911, reissued in Nordisk Historia in 1948, the Swedish professor Lauritz Weibull took it upon himself to teach his Danish and Norwegian colleagues a lesson in the methods of historical inquiry. His own views on the subject of Rollo's descent and nationality are summed up in the following passage: "All we can determine historically is that Dudo and tradition after him in Normandy turned the rather vague Dacia into the homeland of Rollo and his men. This tradition is the oldest, a century younger than Rollo. At the same time Northmannia and Northmanni, the earlier names of the northern countries and the Northmen, had developed, on the one hand, into "Norway and Norwegians," and on the other, into "Normandy and Normans." As early as the 11ᵗʰ century the foundation of Normandy is attributed to Norway, and in the next century Rollo is expressly mentioned as a Norwegian. By the combination of an Irish and an Icelandic tradition Rollo is turned into the Viking, who at the time of Harald Fair-Hair raided Viken, and having been banished won a new country in Normandy." But, as we shall see presently, there are several other important points, which have escaped the attention of the learned professor.

Rollo Dux Dannorum or Northmannorum, a Sea King and a French Count, appears in the chronicles under many different names: Hrolf the Ganger, Gange-Rolf, Gange Rolf, Gange-Hrolfr, Hrolleifus, Going Rolf, Rolvo, Rolfus, Rolus, Roleff, Reolfus, Roes, Rodeo, Rodla and Rosus. The name given to him on becoming a Christian was Robert (Robertus, Rodbertus). He seems also to have been given several cognomens such as Haesten, and Hunedanus (corrupted from Hunedeus and Huncdeus) with special stress on his nationality as an Orkney Dane. In the isle of Gotland he was known as Roes, and as a native of Moere, he was called Moericus.

1. HAESTEN

Addressing the General Assembly of the *Société de l'Histoire de Normandie* on 28ᵗʰ July, 1880, the honorary president of that illustrious society made the following reference to the *Norman Chronicles*:

"Gentlemen, the Norman Chieftain Rolle had hardly transformed himself into a French duke [it should be count], when a monk, whose name remains unknown tried to outline a consecutive history of the Scandinavian invasions of France. This gifted scientist put his hands on several excellent chronicles, the Annales of Eginard, of Saint Bertin, of Saint Waast and also other chronicles of later date. He transcribed from each of them the passages dealing with the facts and acts of the Normans, and out of these extracts he made up the work known as the Norman chronicles (de Normanum Gestis de Francia)."

This work contains the following passage referring to Rollo: "Notre dus Hastens qui Sarrazins est (which meant pirate or Viking), et nee de Danemarche."

This statement shows that Rollo was also called Hastens and that he was born in a territory under the Danish crown. At that time, Hesten or Heesten was a common name in Sleswig; compare also Hengist, the Anglo-Saxon conqueror.

Another instance: The siege of Tours from 883-5 has been described in several chronicles. Most of them call the Norman chieftain on this occasion Hastens, or Haesten, but Monachus Floriacensis makes Rollo the leader of the operations, because he was known under both names. Ivar, the son of Ragnar/Reginfrid, was also known under his surname, Bagsaeg. The Saxon chronicles and Florence of Worcester call him Haesten, which in Danish means horse. But he is also called Ganger, the other Danish word for horse. There might have been some truth in the old saying that this heavy chieftain could not find a horse strong enough to carry him, so he fought on foot. In other words, he was his own horse (haest, ganger). All this makes Rollo's story much more comprehensible. A great Viking chief of his qualities, who achieved such far reaching and lasting results, could not have passed unknown to the Norman historians and chroniclers until 911 when he made his first appearance in contemporary works under the name Rollo. It seems incredible that he should have arrived for the first time in Normandy the year before the country was handed over to him. There is no reason why we should not believe the very definite statement in the chronicles that "Rollo and his band landed in Normandy on the fifteenth of the calends of December 876," twenty-six years earlier.

It is most important also to place on record that William of Malmesbury quotes the following statement of William the conqueror: "Hastinagus, antecessorum nostrum" (Haesten, our ancestor). It seems obvious that King William here referred to the founder of the Norman dynasty, Rollo.

2. HUNEDANUS

The Hunaland of the *Edda* has often been identified with Saxony, but we (B. G. Montgomery & myself) have found no facts to support this statement. To judge by the linguistic toponymy, Hunaland must be the ancient Scandinavian name for the north of Scotland and the Orkneys and be connected with the tribe of Canine-fates, who settled in those parts. They had the dog as their totem, hence their Latin name. In their own language the Latin *canis*, the English *dog or hound*, the Danish *hund* and the Icelandic *hunde*, was *huna*. The names *Hundeus* and *Hunedeus* in the French chronicles are a Latinization of Hunde. In other words, he was called The Danish wolf or the Danish Wolf-hound.

The Chatti (who had the cat as their totem, hence the word chat, cat and of course Clan Chattan, the Clan of the Cats) have given their name to Caithness, where they settled long before the Gaelic invasion of Scotland. The Canine-fates were a continental tribe of Chatti who once occupied the Ruhr valley. In the time of the Emperor Julianus they were attacked and defeated by the Romans and their country was placed under Roman domination about A.D. 400. This tribe eventually found refuge among their kinsmen, the Chatti of

Scotland. On old Latin maps we find the names Canisbay, Canenesby and Caninusby in Caithness. On old English maps Canisbay is given its Chattic name Huna Bay, which means the same thing, and we find both Huna Inn and Huna Ness in Canisbay parish. Hunda Island amongst the Orkneys also reminds us of the Canine-fates, but the name appears in its Danish form.

In order to distinguish the Danes of the Orkney Islands from those of Jutland and Lethre, they seem to have been called *Hunedani*. It should be noted in this connection that the large estates in Suffolk, recorded in the *Domesday Book* as Hunedana and Hunendana, were held by Rollo's lineal descendant, Richard Comte de Brionne, a great-grandson of Richard I.

One must bear these facts in mind when considering the following statements in the chronicles:

1. In *Annals Vedastine* A.D. 895-6 we read: "At the same time the Northmen with their Duke whose name was Hunedeus with five barges entered the Seine... the Northmen in increased numbers entered the Oise shortly before Christmas."

2. *Chron. de Gestis Norm. in Francia* A.D. 895 (ed. Duchesne) has recorded the same expeditions but calls the leader Rollo: "The Northmen again with their Duke, who is named Rollo, entered the Seine, and before Christmas day moved up the Oise with their numbers increased."

3. *Chron. Rerum Septrionalium* refers to the same events but calls the leader Rodo.

Now it often happened with the Vikings, who had been baptized, that they returned to their Odonic faith after a time, and this was apparently the case with Rollo.

Annales Vedastini A.D. 896 state: "Charles indeed raised up Huncdeus from the font." The form "Huncdeus" in these Annales is undoubtedly a corruption. *Sigebertus Gemblaciensis* refers to the same event: "King Charles caused Hunedeus, King of the Northmen to be baptized and raised him up from the font."

These statements seem to indicate that Rollo was baptized twice, since he had to undergo the same procedure in pursuance of the treaty of Saint-Clair-sur-Epte in 912. Some chronicles state that he had a second relapse and sacrificed a hundred victims to Thor and Woden before his death in order to appease the anger of these dreaded and perhaps also beloved gods of his ancestors. Perhaps he never really became a Christian!

The name Hunedanus was quite in keeping with Chattic and Visigothic practice. It would indicate that he was an Orkney Dane and more especially that his father was of Danish and his mother of Chattic descent. His full name was Rollo Hunedanus, *alias* Haesten. Before his first christening he seems to have been generally known under either of his surnames and we may therefore assume that his first Christian name was Rollo. On the occasion of his second baptism, the name of the relapsed pagan had to be changed and he was given that of his sponsor Robert, Duke of France, second son of Robert le Fort. Though styled officially Robert I, Count of Rouen, he was known to the world as Rollo, Duke of the Normans.

3. MOERICUS

Saemundre Sigfuson, the first of the Icelandic historians (1056-1133), is said to have travelled abroad. He probably visited both London and Paris. During his studies he no doubt had access to a copy of Dudo's history of Normandy (*Acta Normannorum*), completed before 1026. The passage in which Dudo describes the conqueror of Normandy as *Rollo Moericus* must then have caught his eye and the Icelander may well have jumped to the conclusion that Rollo must have been connected in some way with Söndmör, south west of Trondhjem. We may assume that this information was passed on to his successors among the storytellers of Iceland, Are Frode, Snorre Sturluson, Sturla Thorvarson, Sturme and Haukr, and that the whole story of Gangfu Hrolfr in Snorre's saga was constructed around Dudo's statement. As a matter of fact, there is no evidence to prove that there was a province of Moere or even Söndmör in Norway at the time of Rollo, nor indeed that a jarl of Moere by the name of Ragnvald has ever existed. The whole story of Snorre is extremely inconsistent and must be treated with the utmost circumspection. This applies also to *Heimskringle*, according to which the fabulous Moere Jarl was murdered by some of King Harald's sons.

Snorre spent a long time at the court of the Norwegian King, Haakon Haakonson. He is known to have been very avaricious and there is no doubt that parts of his Sagas were written under the influence of drink. Fables and other products of wild imagination are mixed with historical facts into a magic brew. Yet Snorre has an extraordinary faculty of presenting fiction as facts in a manner that looks convincing. Errors are therefore better hidden than in the works of Richerius and Dudo, whence his better reputation with those historians who recognise only superficially his methods of research and his art of presenting the offshoots of his sick mind as true facts. A summary of the mistakes, intentional or unintentional, in Snorre's sagas would fill volumes. Only a few are mentioned here.

As a general observation it may be said that he had the Icelander's deeply rooted hatred of the kings of Norway at the back of his mind when writing their history, even though he was dependent on their bounty. His description of the matrimonial affairs of Harald Fair Hair is gruesome and distasteful and he deprived that great monarch of his true genealogy, turning him into a descendant of Ingiald the Malevolent, whereas his true progenitor was Herioldus Brochus, *alias* Hylthetan. This deliberate and insidious falsification of facts may have been the reason why Snorre was eventually murdered, probably at the instigation of the Norwegians. The imaginary king Ivar Widefathom, who should have lived four generations before the equally imaginary Ragnar Lothbroc, is turned into a contemporary of Helge Vasse, whose mother was Ragnar's grand-daughter – a gap of seven generations.

Harald Fair Hair was born about 860. Snorre states that he conquered Trondheim five years later, aged 5!! He has fathered upon this king twenty-three sons. Among these are recorded Torgils and Frode, who conquered the seat of Dublin in 838, i.e. twenty-two years before the birth of their supposed father!

Even in the case of more recent events, he gives his imagination free play. Thus he tells us the following story of William the Conqueror: "The day he mounted his horse to ride from the castle to his ships, his wife came forward to speak to him. When he saw this he kicked her with his heel so that the stirrup penetrated her chest and she fell down dead on the spot. But the Earl rode to the ships and embarked with his army for England." (As we know; Queen Mathilda was crowned in London in 1068 and her son John was born the same year. She died in 1083, seventeen years after the conquest.)

Let us hope that these examples may be enough to prove that Snorre Sturluson is not entitled to be quoted as an authority against Dudo and Richerus.

The *Landnámabók*, which was partly compiled under the personal supervision of Snorre, must be treated with the same cautious scepticism. The detailed pedigrees, which seem to be worked out with great precision, are most impressive, but are in many cases sheer inventions. Thus for instance all the pedigrees from Queen Aud Djup-Udga (The Very Rich) must be ruled out. Aud Djup-Ugda was the imaginary daughter of the imaginary king Ivar Widefathom and was certainly not married to King Olaf the White of Dublin, who lived two centuries later than these personalities are alleged to have flourished. The wife of this king is known from the Irish chronicles. He married Ligach, only daughter of Aodh Finlaith, King of Erin, and Maolmhuire, daughter of Kenneth, King of Scotland. After Olaf's death, Ligach married Congal, King of Erin. The compilers of the *Landnámabók* have apparently turned the Irish king Aodh into a queen, who was made the ancestral mother of many settlers in Iceland.

They must have mistaken the genitive of the king's name for a woman's name and translated *Aodhs* daughter* (see below, *The Three Fragments* in Gaelic and its translation) into *daughter Audlha*, which makes a great difference. The whole story of Queen Aud Djup-Udga and all her descendants is nothing but a fraud originally based on a false transliteration.

The same compilers have seen to it that Rollo left a daughter in Scotland from whom many settlers in Iceland claim descent. The French, Saxon and Irish chronicles know nothing about this offspring of the Norman duke. She may have existed, but from the point of view of historical research it seems more correct to make her keep company with Queen Aud the Very Rich and to regard her merely as a subject of Snorre's vivid imagination. The same judgement must be passed on Ragnvald of Moere and all his imaginary sons. Thanks to the Norwegian explorer Wulstan's report to King Alfred, however, we know with absolute certainty that a territory with name of Moere existed at the time of Rollo, not in Norway, but in what is now the Swedish province of Småland. This territory might be included in Dudo's ambiguous expression Dacia, as having a population of Visigoths, whom Dudo, like the Greek historians, would identify with the Getae of the Roman province Dacia on the bank of the Danube. In the Middle Ages, the Scandinavian students at the University of Paris were grouped under the heading Daciae.

At the time of Rollo, there were strong fortified places both in Moere and in Öland that seem to have formed the nucleus of a military base for the defence of the Baltic region. The fact is that the same kings ruled both over this base and over the extremely important strategic base, which is now known under the name of Scapa Flow. We shall return to this question presently in connection with our search for the father and grandfather of Rollo. Since Rollo's territories stretched from the Orkney Islands to the Baltic country of Moere, Dudo had as good a right to call him "Moericus," as other French chroniclers to give him the name Hunedanus.

Snorre tells us that the fabulous Moere Jarl, Rollo's pretended father, was Harald's dearest friend. It does not seem likely, therefore, that his son descended on Viken as an enemy and was then outlawed by the king and expelled from Norway. If Rollo ever raided Viken it is far more probable that he did this in order to establish a claim of inheritance or to avenge some wrong he had suffered. This again, would suggest that Rollo or the family to which he belonged had held that province. Finally, there is no reason to believe that Harald ever conquered Viken.

In order to improve Snorre's story, some writers have identified the Viken to which he refers with places within near reach of Söndermöre. Thus Thomas Carlyle writes, "Rolf, son of Rognvald, was lord of three little inlets far north, near the fjord of Folden, called the three Vigten Islands." But even this explanation does not make Snorre's version any more digestible to a modern historian. On many occasions Snorre has referred to Viken and it is quite clear from the context that he means the province on the west coast of Sweden, which was called Ranrike or Ragnarike and is now called Bohuslän.

* Cp. The Three Fragments of the Annals of Ireland for 862.

Αοὸ mαc Νέιll ˥ α cliαṁαιn .ι. Ⱥmlαɓ (ιngⁱⁿ Ⱥοὸα ɼο ɓαοι
αȝ Ⱥṁlαοιɓ) ȝο ɼloȝαιɓ móɼα Ȝαοιὸιol ˥ ⱡοⱡlαnn leo ȝο mαȝ
mιὸe, ˥ α ιοnnɼαὸ leo, ˥ ɼαοɼⱡlαnnα ιοmὸα ὸο ṁαɼɓαὸ leo.

(Translation: Aedh, son of Niall, and his son-in-law, i.e. Amblaeibh (the daughter of Aedh was wife to Amhlaeibh) set out with great forces of Gaeidhil and Lochlanns to the plain of Meath, and they plundered it and slew many noble persons.).

4. ROES (or Rhoes or Rollo)

The Roes stone in the parish of Grötlingbo in the Baltic island of Gottland has long been considered as an unsolvable riddle. If, however, we regard it as an illustration of a certain event in Rollo's life, then perhaps we can ascertain its meaning.

Archaeologists have not, so far as I am aware, been able to ascertain the period to which this stone belongs, but it might very well be a product of the ninth century. It depicts a horse chased by a bird, possibly the hawk of Uôuin or the raven of Woden. What is then the connection between this petroglyph and Rollo? The answer is that the great Viking chieftain was alternately called Roes (in Gottland russ, which means horse), Haesten (which is Danish for horse), and Ganger (which is another Danish word for horse), and that the stone depicts the scene when Rollo, for some reason or other, was driven out of the country by the king, possibly Anund.

This monument is in sandstone and quite small, only 33 x 22 x 3.5 inches. The inscription in Runic letters reads: "iudh (Udu, Uduin, Odin, Gud) I(a) g(a)r r(oes) h(äste)n" (Woden drives out Roes the Horse). So Rollo is driven out by the King, representative of Woden! Why? Perhaps because he had accepted baptism and was no longer the representative of Woden as he had been!

It has been suggested that this stone simply reads, "Roes drew this horse of Odin."

Appendix IV

Rollo's Father

Keitel's (Askettil's) Son

Dudo, dean of Saint-Quentin, who wrote the first history of Normandy, was rather an historiographer than a historian. He served three masters: Richard I of Normandy, known as Sans-Peur, who entrusted him with the task of writing it, his son Richard II, and Bishop Adelbéron of Laon, who attended to the interests of the Church and scrutinized his manuscript. He began to write in 994 A.D.

His chief informant was Raoul d'Ivry, uterine brother of Richard-sans-Peur, whose mother Sprota married secondly Asperleng de Vaudreuil, Raoul's father. Although not himself a descendant of Rollo, Raoul's father showed great interest in the history of the Norman dynasty to which he was so closely related through his mother. We may reasonably assume that he knew the names of Rollo's father and grandfather but that for some reason or other, after consulting his brother, decided that these names should not be made public; and that consequently, he instructed Dudo to that effect. It was certainly not in the interest of the Duke to make the clergy aware of the direct affiliation of the Ducal house to Bier Costae Ferrae or any other Viking chief whose acts of violence were fresh in the memory, and particularly if they claimed descent, not only from Odin, but also from the Davidic line of Jesus.

That Dudo found himself in a precarious position appears clearly from the following passage in the preface to his book. "It is what he (Raoul) has told me that I have written in this book with mixed feelings – surprised, shaking, stupefied, frightened, doubtful." *Small wonder for a monk to find that your patron claims descent from Jesus himself!* On the other hand, it shows that Dudo felt his responsibility to posterity notwithstanding that he wrote under instruction. It must be recognized that *De moribus et actis primorum Normanniae ducum* is primarily the work of Raoul d'Ivry, even if Dudo has wielded the pen.

It seems a pity that several relevant facts have been excluded for political reasons. Those we have received must therefore be studied with all the more attention whilst always keeping in mind that the source of information is the Ducal house itself. We shall attempt to deal with a few of them.

Dudo does not give the name of Rollo's father. He only refers to him as an Oriental Potentate in the following terms: "Erat enim omnium Orientalium...

praepotentissimus." Dudo has been criticised for this statement but those who criticise only show their own ignorance. They forget or do not seem to know of the Scandinavian rulers in Russia, which, to the people of Dudo's time, were certainly judged *oriental*. As we shall see presently, Dudo's reference to Rollo's father seems quite in keeping with the historical background.

The chronicles of Nantes have made the following annotation for the year 876: "Rollo duke of the Normans disembarked on the coast of Gaul," and Dudo has this version of the venture:

"In the year 876 A.D. and since he had conferred with his confidants the noble Rollo set sail and left, with the wind aft, the mouth of the river Schelde in order to travel by sea to the point where the blue water of the river Seine discharges....

He penetrated with his fleet of hostile ships as far as Jumiéges. The impoverished people and the little merchants who were prevented from continuing their trade at Rouen on account of his occupation of the river, and all inhabitants of this district who had been informed that a well-armed force of Northmen had reached Jumiéges, came to see Franco, bishop of Rouen, in order to discuss with him what measures should be taken."

Dudo's critics have pointed out that the name of the bishop of Rouen at that time was not Franco, but Johannes, and that consequently the whole of Dudo's version of the events connected with Rollo's first invasion of Normandy must be inaccurate. Such a sweeping judgement on grounds so flimsy is unjustifiable. We must not forget that one of King Charles's most intimate friends and his councillor was Franco, Bishop of Tongres, who having been informed of Rollo's dedparture from Schelde, left for Rouen in order to organize the defence. It seems likely therefore, that Dudo simply mistook Johannes for Franco, who in fact became Bishop of Rouen at a somewhat later date.

The Anglo-Saxon chronicle (MS Domitian A. VIII) contains an interpolation stating that Rodla penetrated into Normandy in A.D. 876. Benjamin Thorpe, the editor of this chronicle, makes the following reference to this note: "The date of Rolf's landing in France seems to be correctly given, at least it accords with Ordericus Vitalis and Florence of Worcester." The point is that this expedition was Rollo's *first landing* in Normandy.

Probably on the authority of the Norman chronicles, Florence of Worcester states that, "Rollo and his followers landed in Normandy on the fifteenth of the calends of Dec. (17th Nov.) 876." This passage has been copied by other chroniclers and Mathew, Archbishop of Canterbury, seems to be responsible for its interpolation in the manuscript used for his printed edition of Bishop Asser's *Life of King Alfred* (1574). Many historians have been misled into thinking that this interpolation formed part of the original manuscript of Bishop Asser, who was a contemporary of Rollo's. In a note to his Oxford edition of Asser's work, published in 1904, William Stevenson writes: "Many difficulties have arisen from the acceptance of this date of the *settlement* of Rollo in Normandy, which is obviously wrong." Stevenson is right in stating that the settlement did not take place at that time, but he is decidedly not entitled to dismiss this important passage on such a ground; because it does not refer to a settlement, but merely to a first landing of Rollo's forces in Normandy. Even if this passage was interpolated at a later date in Archbishop Mathew's edition of Asser's work, it must be recognized that it was based on almost contemporary evidence, which the editor was prepared to accept.

There is no doubt that Rollo made a descent on Neustrie in 876 with that part of the Viking army which left England after the first conclusion of peace between King Alfred and King Athelstan, *alias* Guthrum, and that his invasion was somewhat delayed, owing to the fact that his fleet had been wind-driven onto the Isle of Walcheren. It should be noticed that before the appearance of the Icelandic story writers, it was generally recognized that Rollo made his first attack on France in 876. The Norman and Saxon chronicles present a united front on this point. The Norwegians did not appear in French waters until more than thirty years later. In order to comply with the wish of Icelandic writers, historians who were impressed by the statements of these self-confident charlatans, promptly dismissed the evidence produced by the much older chronicles, accordingly postponing the time for Rollo's first invasion of France. But since the Earl of Moere and his many sons and earldom are simply phantoms of a lively imagination, we had better stick to the more reliable and contemporary sources of the monks' chronicles. After all, they were the ones whose monasteries got sacked and should know better than most when this happened.

Richerus (Richerius, Richer), a Benedictine monk of Saint-Remi at Rheims, wrote the continuation of Hincmar's famous annals dealing with the latter part of the Viking Age. He was Dudo's contemporary, but in contrast to Dudo he was under no restrictions on his work for the sake of the Norman dukes. He even called Rollo a pirate prince. His father was a warrior in the service of the French king, Louis d'Outremer, and lived very near the time of Rollo. He belonged to the king's bodyguard and distinguished himself during the assaults on Laon and Mons. We might expect that he had a good deal to tell his son about the Norman duke, which makes the history of Richerus a work of first rate importance. Even if he may be wrong in some of his facts, the information he gives is of far superior quality to that of the Icelandic stories. It must be treated with reverence and should never be dismissed without clear evidence of its inaccuracy. His manuscript was discovered by Pertz at the beginning of the last century in the cathedral library of Bamberg.

Richerus makes Rollo the son of Catillus. He writes: "Irruperanty enim duce Rollone, *filio Catilli*, intra Neustriam repenti, anno 911." The interpolation, here in italics, has been added later, but experts seem to be of the opinion that it is written in Richer's hand.

In his book quoted above, le Marquis de Saint-Pierre makes the surprising statement that Richerus has given Rollo the Viking, Kettil of the Hebrides, as father. On the next page he declares that Richerus, according to an old tradition from Chartres, made Kettil, Count of the Hebrides, (killed at Limoges 892) Rollo's father. These allegations do not give Richerus a fair chance, for statements have been attributed to him that he had never made. There is not a word in his chronicles about either the Viking Kettil or the Count Kettil of the Hebrides. Fascinated by the Icelandic pedigrees, which have the appearance of trustworthiness, the author of *Rollon devant l'Histoire* has been carried away by his own thoughts and by his clearly demonstrated conviction that Catillus, mentioned by the Benedictine monk, could be none other than the Icelanders' Kettil Flatnoze. Yet Godfrid, son of Feargus, is styled chief of Fingall in 835 and chief of the Isles in 851 (*Annals of the Four Masters*). Moreover, Olav, King of Denmark, is designated king of the land in Ireland called Fingall in 832 (*Annals of Clonmacnois 829*). This does not give room for the imaginary figure of "Kettil le Camus, roi des Isles."

In France and England, Rollo's descent from Bjorn Ironside is supported by a very strong tradition. Robert Wace opened his versified history of the Dukes of Normandy with a great epic glorifying this Viking king. It seems quite clear from the context that Wace, and no doubt his informants about the middle of the twelfth century, considered Bjorn as the ancestor of Rollo.

An ancient document in Bibl. Royale in Paris (MS. Latin 5195 published by Francisque Michel) contains the following statement translated from Latin into Old French: "Rou premier duc de Normandie fu native de Dannermarche, filz [in the sense of descendant] d'un trés noble et puissant homme nommé Bierte Coste-Serrée, séigneur de Yrd et de Boure, qui sont deux grands terres et seigneuries en royaume de Dannemarche."

The lands recorded in the above manuscript are not to be found in Denmark proper, but in the Danish dependencies of that period, the Orkneys and Caithness. Sutherland is divided from Caithness by the river Ord and Burray is an island in the Orkneys. This island commands the entry to the Scapa Flow, the finest harbour in Europe, excellently situated from a strategical point of view. It is no wonder that Raghnall and his sons had chosen just this spot from which to launch their formidable raids on any coast of Europe. The name Boure also recalls the name Burs in Gotland. The parish of Groetlingbo, where the Roes Stone was raised, is situated between Burs and Bursvik. These places may have had the character of *Terra Regis* held by the house of Lothbroc.

In 1840 Michel published another ancient document, which throws some light on Rollo's descent (*Histoire des Ducs de Normandie et des Rois d'Angleterre*). The first part of this manuscript is also a translation from older Latin documents. The following quotation is particularly interesting in this connection:

"Puis montepliierent tant li Danois en la tierre de Dannemarche que derechief ler convint jeter en escil. En la tierre avoit eu novielment mort .i. haut homme qui avaoit à non Bier Coste-Fierrée. Dues fils avaoit: Roule et Burin...."

If the original manuscript, as appears from the text, dates back from the time when Bier had recently died, it cannot have been written later than the beginning of the tenth century and in the life-time of Rollo. That his brother bore the Russian name Burin (Burins), which means Bjorn, makes it more likely that he was the grandson but not the son of Bjorn. Consequently, one generation is missing. This gap, as we have seen, has been covered by Richerus. We are now in a position to sum up the principal points of the chronicles and manuscripts under review.

- Dudo makes it clear that Rollo's father was an oriental potentate.

- Richerus gives his name in Latin – Catillus.

- His name in the Saxon chronicles is Oscetil, which in Swedish is Asakettil and in Russian Ascold.

- The Nordic chieftain who was duke of Kiev about 880 bore the name of Ascold. To call him an oriental potentate would be correct.

- There was an irresistibly strong tradition in France and England centuries before the Icelandic story-tellers appeared on the scene, that Rollo descended from Bjorn Ironside and that his first descent on Neustrie took place in 876.

- Archbishop Mathew's interpolation in Bishop Asser's manuscript was misleading from a bibliographical point of view, but historically sound. Dudo gave Rollo the surname Moericus, indicating that he was born in the hundred of Moere and that his father was at the time a petty-king of that part of south Sweden.

- Snorre has caused much confusion by his statement that the sons of Harald Fair Hair, Togils and Frode, were the first Vikings who conquered Dublin. We know now with certainty that Harald was not born, still less his sons, when the Danish chieftains Turges and Frotho performed that deed, which was in 838.

- Ketil Flatnose of Llandnáma fame belongs to the same class of unhistorical personalities. All we know about him is that as a contemporary of Harald's sons, he would have been at least seventy years younger than his supposed son-in-law; that Olav the White did not marry his daughter; that her name was not Aud-the-Very-Rich; that owing to an error of translation, the compilers of the Landnáma book mistook the Irish King Aodh or Aedh for a queen whom they called Auda; that Kettil Flatnose was never king of the Isles nor Count of the Hebrides, and that consequently we must regard him as a product of vivid Icelandic imagination.

These circumstances must be taken into consideration when we have to judge the value of Richerus as an historian in comparison with the Icelandic writers of several centuries later. The criticism launched by le Marquis de Saint-Pierre is very largely based on the Icelandic stories about Kettil, Aud and Rollo's invented bastard child in Scotland. This makes the position of Richerus all the stronger. If criticism must be based on such evidence and on arguments as weak, there is no reason whatsoever to doubt the truth of Richerus's statement that the name of Rollo's father was *Catillus*. Richerus, a contemporary of Richard Sans-Peur and of his son and successor Richard le-Bon, born nearly two centuries before the Icelander Snorre in a civilized country, was an extremely well informed man and was not, like Dudo, under the influence of the Norman dukes. Even if, now and then, he allowed his imagination free play, he must be regarded as a first rate authority and his evidence weights heavily "jusqu' à preuve du contraire."

It seems natural to look for Catillus in the first instance among the descendants of Brochus, who were the leaders of all the big Viking raids in Ireland, England and France. It is important to note that several of these kings and jarls figure at the same time as Danes, Norwegians, Swedes or Russians, since their dominions covered territories in several of these countries. Thus for instance the kings of Westfold in Norway were equally kings in Jutland, and kings of Upsala were sometimes kings of Lethra, and some kings in Sweden were also lords of Hedeby in south Jutland. The Irish used the vague term "king of Lochlann" to designate alternately Danish, Norwegian and Swedish kings.

We meet the house of Lothbroc for the first time in a body during their invasion of Ireland, which seems to have taken place about 833. *The Annals of Clonmacnois* give the names of the chief captains of the invading force. The leader of the expedition seems to have been Awuslir. We are here confronted with no less a person than Bjorn Ironside himself. Awuslir is an Irish distortion of Latin Ursival and Slavonic Surislav, which means "the great bear." He is undoubtedly identical with the only historically established king with this name in Scandinavia at that time, Bjorn-at-Haugi, who was King of Upsala and resided at Birka during St. Anscharius's visit to that place in 829.

It is in this company we recognise Rollo's father for the first time. His name in the Irish annals is alternately Osil, Osceytil, Oscetyl; in Saxon Oscytel, Oskytel. Os is Gaelic for Nordic Asa, a designation suggesting descent from the deified kings of Norse Mythology (the Odonic Line – See *God Kings of Europe*, Chap. 1). His full name in Swedish would be Asakettil, in some chronicles contracted into Askell. This chieftain was apparently well-known to the Irish chronicler who has recorded him as "Ossil and the sons of Imar."

Besides Bjorn and Oscetyl we find Bjorn's brother Sigfrid (cognomen Frotho, Fatha), who was King of Denmark when parts of England were conquered and therefore was honoured with the further cognomen, Anglicus. Other warriors who served in this expedition were:

a) Baron Robert, no doubt Robert-le-Fort, son of Theodebert or Thibaut, seigneur de Matrie, son of the Saxon chieftain Widukind, d. 812, and the Danish princess Gheva, which explains his taking part in the Danish expedition; Count of Anjou and ancestor of the Capetian dynasty, 866.

b) Turges, identified with Raghnaill (Ragnvald) Godfridson, conqueror of Paris in 845, younger brother of King Horic, killed in Ulster, 847.

c) Awley, identified with Olav Godfridson, King of Denmark.

d) Imer, Ingvar son of Godfrid, King of Vestfold, King of Dublin, 872.

e) Imer, Ivar, son of Raghnall Halvdanson, brother of Frotho and Bjorn, killed 871.

f) Dowegean (Gaelic for Chattic Hund), Mac Dowgean is an Old Norse *Hunding*, cf. Cadowgean, contracted Cadogan, means Cat-Dog i.e. Lion-Dog.

g) Ottar Duff (d'Uff for Ulvung) cf. family Mac Duff, and Torbert Duff, probably a younger son.

h) Goslyn, cp. Gauzlin, the bishop who defended Paris in 885, and Gosceline, Abbot of St. Germain-des-Près, fl 889. Goslyn from Gosling, young goose.

Goslyn, Swanchean (Swanshield) and Griffin (Gripen) bore apparently heraldic figures on their shields. This is important to notice, since it is generally held that the first heraldic arms of chivalry appeared in France about 1150, i.e. after the second crusade and under Oriental influence. However, some of the heraldic names mentioned in connection with the Danish invasion of Ireland seem to suggest that the Vikings, who had frequent connections with Greece and Persia, had adopted heraldic figures well over three centuries earlier. The griffin (Lat. gryphus) was used as a symbol among the Hittites more that 2000 years B.C. and the goose as a symbol was known in the Sumerian kingdom of Mesopotamia even before that time. Here is yet another item showing the connection of the Odonic line with ancient Messopotamia. By the Vikings, they were originally used for military purposes as the marks of a special *hundred*, or gaelic *clan*.

Many writers have committed the mistake of identifying the "black foreigners," *Dubh-Galls*, with the Danes and the "white foreigners," *Finn-Galls*, with the Norwegians. These designations may have referred to hair and complexion or to the black or white shields carried by the warriors in battle, but it should be clearly understood that there were fair men among the Danes and dark men among the Norwegians. It was not until after the union of Norway about A.D. 900 that a distinction between Danes and Norwegians became possible. The Swedish Vikings were also both dark and fair.

Oscytel (Askytel, Auscatil, Asaketil) was with the Danish forces at Repton in 875 and is expressly styled a king in the chronicles. In the same year, he broke away from Repton with two other kings — Guthrum, the son of Frotho, King of Denmark, and Anund, king in Sweden, and marched south. They eventually settled at Cambridge and took possession of Wessex. According to Dudo and other Norman chroniclers, Rollo took part in the ensuing campaign of these kings against King Alfred. In 876, Guthrum signed a treaty with Alfred which bound him to become a Christian, but Asaketil, Rollo and Anund refused to comply with this condition and sailed for Normandy in Nov. 876.

Oscytel commanded the Danish troops in the Allier district, but his forces were completely routed by the French king, Odo, in 890. According to Richerus, the Danish king was taken prisoner and removed to Limoges. The story of his subsequent murder seems incoherent and generally incredible. We shall return to this question presently.

There is not the slightest doubt that this Oscytel (Asakettil) is the chieftain Richerus called Catillus and marked out as father of Rollo. Who was, then, Oscytel's father, Rollo's grandfather?

Bjorn Ironside   [O. Swed. Biorn Jársniòa, O. French Bier-Costae-Ferrae, Slavonic Burislaw, Latin Ursival, Irish Awuslir] a lineal descendant of Herioldus Brochus, was the greatest of all Viking kings. We can fathom vaguely the outlines of his empire and we know several of his campaigns from contemporary chronicles.

Annales Bartholiniani call him *Lothbroci Regis filius*, owing to a misunderstanding of the name Lothbroci [it would better read Loth Broci Rex]. Robert Wace styles him *fiz du Lothbroc un Danois Roy* (would better read *stirps [or fiz in the sense of descendant] de Brocus un Danois Roy*). There is no statement in the chronicles to the effect that his father was identical with Raghnall of the Orkneys, but we may draw this conclusion from the following facts:

The *Irish Fragments* make it clear that Raghnall was chief of the Aunites, and the forces which destroyed York in 869 (apparently in revenge for Raghnall's death) were Aunites i.e. Visigoths; the forces of Bjorn Ironside in France were called Visigoths (Fraga. Mirac. S. Bercharii); contemporary chronicles make Bjorn the commander of the Viking raids in the Mediterranean countries recorded in the *Irish Fragments* as the deeds of the older sons of Raghnall

Most chronicles concur in making Bjorn Ironside a king in Sweden (presumably as a Danish overlord) and since the only contemporary king in that country with that name was Biorn-at-Haga, who received St. Anscharius on his first visit to Birka in 829. Logically, therefore, one can identify this king with Bjorn, afterwards famous under the cognomen of Ironside.

In the Baltic island of Öland, there is a huge open stronghold, Gråborg, which, according to tradition, was held by a king called Bugislev (or Burislaw), the Russian name of Bjorn Ironside. It was probably built by Russian soldiers, in the service of one of his ancestors. There is another fortified place at Ismanstorp on the same island. It is somewhat smaller and was built on the pattern of a Khazak *gorodi*. (I pointed out in *The God-Kings of Europe* that the Odonic line probably descended from the Kassite dynasty of Mesopotamia called Kassu, Cassi, Khazar and here is another small item to support this proposition.) The gigantic Torsburgen near the east coast of Gotland is the biggest of all prehistoric strongholds in Sweden. It has an area of about 264 acres, and in times of war the entire population of eastern Gotland could take refuge within the high walls of this masterpiece of 5th century fortifications, built on a calcareous rock.

These three strongholds were apparently the strategic bases of Bjorn Ironside in the Baltic region. From these places he dominated not only the sound of Öland and the great forests of Moere and Blekinge, which furnished the material for his fleets, but also the trade lines to Poland, the Baltic States and Russia.

Already during the Bronze Age there was a considerable trade between Scandinavia and the Orient. The seagoing traffic was almost completely in the hands of Phoenician and Greek merchants, who had good ocean-going ships in great numbers. The river traffic, on the other hand, was largely controlled by the Scandinavians themselves. The river Vistula was an important thoroughfare leading into central Europe, but it was an undertaking fraught with considerable difficulties to reach the Dnieper and the Euxine from the Vistula, by the rivers Prut and Pripet. Moreover, traders would run grave risks of being attacked by warlike tribes all along this route.

As a rule the Sviar used the northern routes, the (Baltic) Dvina, and Berezina and the Dnieper to reach the Euxine, while they used the Neva, Lake

Ladoga and the Wolchow to reach the Volga and the Caspian Sea. Svir, the connecting link between the lakes Ladoga and Onega bears their name. The Scandinavian export comprised chiefly furs, leather, wax, honey and slaves, both men and women. The traders were mostly paid in *drachma*, which helped them to finance and to establish their position along the trade routes where they organized trading centres, collecting annual tributes from the people in the surrounding country. Many of these traders were going in for trade rather than robbery and gained considerable influence. On the other hand, there were Vikings who raided the country through which these caravans passed. On the rivers they had both light boats and barges, and if the caravans were attacked, they were always supported by the men on the river. They made deep inroads into the country in pursuit of game and robbery. Their game was not only furred animals but also men and fair damsels. The latter were, on the whole, treated well and were dressed up in gorgeous costumes in order to fetch top prices in the slave markets of Bulgar and Itil (Astrakan).

Scandinavian colonies were established at Nowgorod, Kieff, Rostov, Smolensk and other places all over central Russia. South Russia was, in the ninth century, in the hands of the Khazars or Khazirs, a people coming from the same parts of Asia as the Kassi and probably of the same origin. They intermarried with Turks, Armenians and Jews. In the middle of the ninth century the Sviar were sufficiently strong enough to establish a central government under the supremacy of the Swedish Crown; and Bjorn Ironside, whose Russian name was Burislaw, was their first *druzhina* (Swedish drott). Upon his death about 862, a Scandinavian prince with the Russian name of Rurik was elected Grand Duke of Nowgorod.

According to Russian chronicles, Rurik was duke in Germany and a vassal of the Roman Emperor. The only prince who answers to this description is Roric, the son of the Danish king Anulo and a cousin of Bjorn Ironside. As a Count of Rustringen, he was a vassal of the Emperor, but he had conquered that country from his future suzerain and was a Christian by name rather than faith. He might have accepted the throne of Nowgorod although it was, at that time, a heathen country. To judge by his record he was a brave man and a great soldier, and it seems likely that the heirs of Bjorn were no match for him and that he wrested Nowgorod from their hands on the death of their father. Rurik was succeeded by Igor (Ingvor), who is said to have been his son, but was probably his grandson, as he died 66 years after him. During Igor's minority Oleg was Regent in Nowgorod. He was a kinsman of Rurik. For the reasons given earlier in this appendix is seems reasonable to assume that the Ascold (Asaketil), who became Duke of Kiev but later on disappeared from the scene. was the son of Bjorn Ironside and identical with Rollo's father Oscytel.

According to the Russian chronicles, Ascold was killed by Oleg because he had become a Christian. This statement recalls the account of his death given by Richerus. In his version, Catillus had been taken prisoner by the French, but King Odo promised to spare his life on condition that he became a Christian. He had refused on other occasions to relinquish the gods of his ancestors. This time he had no other choice and submitted to the condition imposed upon him. The King of France was his sponsor, but after the fact Catillus was viciously attacked by a man called Ingo, said to be the standard-bearer of the king, and killed. When the king reproached Ingo for this foul deed he replied that one could not trust a Saracen (which at that time was synonymous with pirate) and that he had killed him for the sake of the country. The allegation of Richerus that this act was munificently rewarded by the king makes the whole story too fantastic and unbelievable, but part of the storyteller's art at that time was to fuse two traditions. It seems far more probable that Ascold, after his defeat, had returned to Russia and had begun to propagate his new faith. In this situation it seems natural that Oleg should have killed Ascold at the order of Igor (Ingvor) to serve the double object of preventing the spreading of Christianity and of removing a dangerous rival.

Bjorn must have left Russia several years before his death. In 851 he made his first descent on France. Randulphus de Decito has recorded this event under 843, but since this chronicler belonged to the second half of the 12th century and might have been influenced by an unreliable Icelandic source, we must accept the reports of the earlier chroniclers, including William of Jumieges, who have fixed a later date for the event. Prudentius, Bishop of Troyes (whose family-name, like that of the counts of Aragon, was Galindo), wrote the second part of the Annales Bertiniani, covering the years 835-861. Thus, he was contemporary with Bjorn, but has unfortunately only given the year of his departure – 858.

The county of Vermandois in Picardy was first to suffer at Bjorn's hands. He burnt the monastery of Saint-Quentin, devastated the neighbouring districts and perpetrated "the most cruel outrages against the miserable people." He then turned south, seized the town of Noyon, and put the bishop and his deacons to the sword. The whole population of the town was massacred, all in honour of the god Odin and in order to establish his superiority to the God of the Christians. Fresh bands of Vikings collected under his banners and he soon became the virtual "leader" of all the devastation. The town of Rouen was occupied and plundered, whereupon the wild hordes advanced along the Seine in the direction of Paris. The little river island called Oscelle (Osytel) was turned into a fortified camp and a base of operations. The exact position of this island, which apparently was given the name of Bjorn's son and Rollo's father, has been the subject of many learned controversies. Some have placed it near Bourg d'Oissel, not far from Rouen, while others have suggested the neighbourhood of Pont-de-l'Arche, near the point where the river Eure flows into the Seine. It seems more probable, however, that Bjorn selected a place of greater strategical importance near the river Oise. This fact is affirmed by

Prudentius, who tells us that the fortified camp of the Northmen during the winter of 856 was situated at Fossa-Givaldi on the left bank of the Seine, below the confluence of the two rivers. Oscelle must have been an adjacent river-island. The Latin Fossa-Givaldi is, in French, Géfosse, now Jeufosse.

The position of his camp gave Bjorn a firm hold on two main arteries – one essential for the supply of the capital, the other leading into the wheat producing countryside, which would supply the Vikings with all the food they might require. In this way, France would be paralysed and Bjorn would be able to continue his systematic devastation of the country, aiming as he was at the complete extermination of Roman Christianity. Neither churches or monasteries were spared by these terrifying deputies on Earth of Odin. It was only too natural that the French and Norman clergy shuddered at the mere thought of Bjorn Ironside, descendant of Odin and Jesus, being the grandfather of the Norman duke, and should have done their utmost to keep it secret.

After long hesitation and much preparation, Charles-le-Chauve, who afterwards became Emperor, had raised a large army with which he intended to defeat the Vikings. The troops embarked on big barges at Soissons, on which they were taken down the rivers Aine and Oise to the proximity of the Viking camp. After a long siege and blockade, Charles decided to try an assault. The French, however, were beaten off with heavy casualties, and Charles opened negotiations with the enemies in order to persuade them to leave the country. According to Prudentius, these negotiations took place in the Royal palace at Vermeia in 858. Bjorn no doubt received substantial "danegeld" in gold and silver for his promise to leave the country. He also swore fealty to the king, though possibly as representative of the Emperor, which seems to suggest that he received Frisland as a fief under the Imperial crown, because the Emperor was feoffor of that county. The royal army left the barges at the camp and marched back to Soissons. William of Jumieges tells us that Bjorn's fleet met with bad weather in the channel and that many of his ships were sunk. Bjorn got across to Frisland, where he eventually died. This strengthens our assumption that Charles had guaranteed him the possession of this county, which before him had belonged to King Harald of Denmark and his son Godfrid, as vassals of the Emperor.

Bjorn left two sons, Helgi, King of Denmark, father of Gorm Grandaevus and Asakettil (Oscetil, Ascold), King of Moere in Sweden, afterwards Duke of Kiev, father of Rollo.

The following place-names are of interest in this connection, since they recall the names of these princes:

Helgi (Helge) – Helgarum and Helgasjön in Småland, Helgarö in Södermanland, not far from Birka. Helgaville and Heuqueville in

Normandy. These two domains were the properties of the Sires de Toni, according to Ordericus Vitalis "de stripe mala Hulci," i.e. descendants of a daughter of Helgi.

Askakettil – Asa, Aseda, Aasnen in Småland, Asarum in Blekinge and Asige in Halland. Asnelles and Asnières in Normandy.

Ossil, Oscetil – Oscelle, river island in the Seine.

Rollo's cousin, the Danish King Guthrum whose baptismal name was Athelstan, has often been mistaken for King Alfred in the Norman chronicles. Guthrum was King of East Anglia, which he had conquered. The statements in some chronicles that Rollo had made an alliance with King Alfred for united action against the Northmen is certainly not true. On the other hand, we can rest assured that the alliance referred to in the chronicles was a pact with his cousin Guthrum, concluded long before his coming into power in Normandy. This is confirmed by William of Jumieges, who reports that such a pact existed between Rollo and "Alstem," the Christian King of England, ever since 876. It seems obvious that he should refer to the King of East Anglia. This must have taken place about 877 when the major part of the Viking army had left England and Guthrum, with his reduced forces, had to hold his own against the revolting Saxons. William of Jumieges is of the opinion that Rollo was actually at the walls of Paris when receiving Guthrum's message, but this statement is certainly wrong and due to a confusion of dates and events.

After this digression Rollo seems to have returned to his bases in the North, loaded with silver and gold stolen in France and the valuable gifts he had received from Guthrum in recognition of quick and efficient relief. His appearance as a delegate at Constantinople (879) under the name of Rolf Gudi seems to suggest that he had paid a visit to Igor och Oleg in Novgood and to his father, Ascold in Kiev. He had no doubt brought them some of his gifts and impressed them favourable before he was entrusted with this highly important mission.

Rollo and his father eventually returned to France and joined their compatriots who at that time laid siege to Paris under the command of Sigfrid. The newcomers, however, seem to have operated on their own. They seized the town of Meux on the Marne some forty miles N.E. of Paris, afterwards plundering and devastating the rich country of Neustrie between the rivers Seine and Loire. Also on this occasion, Oscetil chose the isle of Oscelle as base for his operations.

In 888 Eudes (Odo), the son of Robert-le-Fort, had been proclaimed King of France after the deposing of Charles-le-Gros. He defeated the main body of the Vikings at Montfaucon on the Meuse, but they escaped complete disaster and soon afterwards renewed their campaign of devastation. Eudes, however, succeeded in his efforts to crush the forces of Oscetil, then operating in the Auvergne. Richerus gives a long and almost too detailed account of the ensuing battle of Montpensier and ends up with the following *crescendo*. "The enemies are losing strength and are thrown back. The Royal army collects itself to a renewed attack, attacks and shatters them. A third blow utterly destroys them. As, towards the end of the tumult, a thick cloud of dust covered the battle-field Catillus managed to escape and to hide with some of his men in a thicket. But his hiding place was discovered by the victorious soldiers who seized him and let his men be put to the sword. Deprived of his clothes he was handed over to the king."

Here follows the combined baptismal and murder scene described above. Trithemius who, like Eckehard, had access to Richerus' manuscript has given a slightly different relation of this event. As we have pointed out already, there is something unreal about this scene, and there is every reason to believe that the murder did not take place on that occasion. I must add another argument for this opinion: Gerlo, Count of Blois, the son of Ingo who was supposed to have committed the crime, was one of Rollo's most intimate friends. It seems highly improbable that the Duke of the Normans would have formed a friendship with his father's murderer.

The explanation seems to be either that Oscetil escaped and joined the other Viking forces or that he was allowed to leave the country on condition that he return to Russia, where he was afterwards murdered. Richerus might in that case have transferred the murder scene from Russia and coupled it with the victory of Montpensier. It is interesting to note that Richerus calls Oscetil a "tyrant," (in its old fashioned meaning of ruler) which is quite in keeping with his position as Duke of Kiev and with the designation "potentate," with which Dudo described Rollo's father.

After Oscetil's disappearance Rollo opened a new campaign, this time in the coastal district of Neustrie. (Dudo has given a detailed description of this campaign.) There are a few words uttered by Rollo at the subsequent peace conference in 911, quoted by Saint-Martins de Tours, which call for special attention. When the Norman chieftain, in accordance with the court-ceremonial, was invited to kiss the foot of the king, he flatly refused, saying: *"ne se bi Got." These words are neither Danish, Swedish nor English, but Anglian* and mean word for word –'"not so, by the gods." Goth is the plural form; the singular is Gota. This statement is important from two points of view. It shows that Rollo still clung to his old gods in the very moment when, at his christening the following year, he was compelled to renounce them. It is also a sign that his mother tongue, the language he spoke when agitated, was Anglian, as spoken by the Hunedanes in the Orkneys.

Many people today, we should say the majority of all those who read about Rollo, labour under the misconception that the whole of Normandy fell to his lot at Saint-Clair-sur-Epte. As a matter of fact, the country ceded to him as a county (Count of Rouen) under the suzerainty of the King of France and was only a minor portion of what afterwards became an independent duchy. The original county was situated north of the Seine, bounded on the south by this river, on the east and northeast by the rivers Epte and Bresle, on the north and northwest by the Channel.

From the start of his reign Rollo was severely handicapped by the circumstance that the whole southern part of Normandy was in the hands of other Danes, centred on the town of Bayeaux. Since they held the coastal district of Calvados, which was particularly well adapted to landing operations with the light craft used by the Danes from England or the mother country, it was well-nigh impossible for Rollo to establish law and order in those parts and to repulse invading forces according to the treaty. Equally serious were the obstacles raised by the heathen neighbours in the path of Christianity.

Hard pressed by Robert, Duke of France, Hugh, his son Raoul, Duke of Burgundy, Robert's son-in-law, and Herbert, Count of Vermandois (who demanded his abdication), Charles-le-Simple appealed to his Norman vassal for support. Rollo promised to bring reinforcements, but on condition that the southern part of Normandy should be added to his fief. The king accepted this condition. Rollo, however, was slow in his preparations and the decisive battle between the king and the duke was fought near Soissons in 923, before Rollo's army had crossed the frontier. The king lost the day and was imprisoned in the castle of Peronne. Robert, Duke of France, was killed in the battle. Hugh was offered the crown but declined, whereupon Raoul was hailed as king.

At this moment, Rollo deemed it expedient to set his troops on the march, breaking into Beauvaisis and Amiènois, plundering and devastating, as was his wont. The town of Beauvais was sacked and Amiens was burned. It was not until he reached Noyon, which was strongly fortified and well defended, that his march was brought to a standstill. Informed by messengers that the Normans had invaded his county, he returned home by forced marches and a strong garrison was put into the fortress of Eu (Lat. *Augae*) on his northern frontier.

He was pursued by the allied army which, however, was not strong enough to venture on a battle since Raoul had returned with his forces to Burgundy. Its leaders, including the Bishop of Rheims, preferred to enter into negotiations. Apparently, Rollo placed his case before them so skilfully that they agreed to his demands for the extension of his territory. For various reasons, they were not willing to include the Maine, although he insisted very strongly on this point. In 925 he opened hostilities to enforce his claim, but on this occasion was defeated by the allied Franco-Burgundian forces, which opened the campaign by a siege of Eu. King Raoul, who was seriously ill, had left the army. Richerus gives the following account of the events, which now ensued.

"After the fortress had been encircled the outworks were carried by assault. Thereupon the young soldiers escaladed the big wall round the town and threw themselves at the enemy. Having occupied the town the soldiers massacred the men, where as the women were saved and protected. The keep was pulled down and burnt. As the fires thickened and darkened the atmosphere many enemies managed to escape and to find their way to an adjacent island. The besiegers attacked and exterminated them in a naval contest. Those pirates who had lost every hope of rescue threw themselves into the water. Some were drowned while others, who tried to swim ashore were massacred by sentries. Even others who had been seized by a dreadful terror tried to take their own lives by their arms."

In the original text, Richerus writes that Rollo had been seized, his eyes had been put out and he had been killed; however, since the learned monk was rather better informed, this passage was expunged. Strangely enough, the heading of the chapter still contains the assertion that Rollo had been killed, but this apparently is due to negligence.

One might have expected that the Normans would be in a difficult position after this disaster, but Rollo was a shrewd diplomat and he soon got his enemies round a conference table. A peace was signed, but the terms are not known. In all probability Rollo waived his claim to the Maine, which remained under the suzerainty of the Crown.

During his last years, the dynastic quarrels in France continued and Rollo was frequently drawn into them. In 927 we find that William Longsword took the place of his old father at a conference with Charles-le-Simple, who had temporarily been released from the prison of Péronne. The Normans suffered another heavy defeat in a pitched battle at Fauquembergue (Falkenberg), not far from Boulogne and St. Omer. King Raoul commanded the French. The exact date of this battle is not known and it seems doubtful whether Rollo was in command on that occasion. Possibly, the report of this last blow ended the life of the great chieftain. Strangely enough, neither Dudo nor Richerus gives the date of his death, which must have taken place between 928 and 930. Since it is generally held that at his death Rollo was eighty years old, he must have been born about 850.

According to Adhémar de Chabannes (writing about 150 years after the death of Rollo), Rollo lost the battle of Limoges to Raoul in 930 and died soon afterwards, abjuring his Christian faith and returning to the cult of Woden or Odin, in proof whereof, he sacrificed 100 prisoners of war to these gods while leaving 100 pounds of gold to the God of the Christians. Notwithstanding this, Rollo was buried in the cathedral of Rouen. The Church, after all, needed to, at the very least, pretend he was a true Christian.

From this investigation into Rollo's family, his names, origin and background, there appears what may be regarded as the following historically established facts:

Dudo designates Rollo as *Moericus*, i.e. from Moere. There is no proof, and it seems unlikely that Dudo knew any other Moere than the Swedish country recorded in Wulfstan's account of his travels, presented to King Alfred at the end of the ninth century. Thus, Rollo was born in that hundred. We can make the assumption that several hundred subjects were perhaps united into a petty kingdom where Rollo's father was the ruling prince.

Dudo makes it clear that Rollo's father was an eastern potentate, a position that he must have held later in life.

Richerus has given his name in Latin – Catillus, in other chronicles, called Oscetil.

The Celtic Os stands for Asa, and his name in Swedish would have been Asakettil, in Russian, Ascold. The Russian prince with that name was a Northman and fits in, chronologically, as Rollo's father. He was Duke of Kiev and as such, would be described as an *eastern potentate*.

Several ancient chronicles and one manuscript copied from a contemporary Latin document state definitely that Rollo was descended from Bjorn Ironside (Bier-costae-ferreae).

Asakettil was the son of Bjorn, which agrees with the fact that he was styled "King" in the Saxon chronicles. Therefore, Bjorn was Rollo's grandfather, and Asakettil his father.

Helgi, King of Denmark, was elder brother of Asakettil and father of Gorm Grandaevus, Rollo's first cousin.

Before he settled in Normandy in 911 Rollo lived the life of a Viking chief, moving from one place to another in the great Empire of the Lodebroci; raiding on his own or taking part in their expeditions, gaining experience and growing in wisdom; qualities which stood him in good stead in protecting his own newly acquired territories.

To the uninitiated observer the Icelandic stories, which are full of entertaining details and of definite statements, have the appearance of reality; but as we have seen, the *Landnámabók* and the *Sagas* of Snorre must be treated with scepticism. They may possess a certain literary value of the heroic mode, but they are largely the products of vivid imagination, misinterpretation and in some cases, falsification of documents. Snorre's stories about the Norwegian kings are marked by his ill feelings towards Norway. His attacks on these kings are insidious and unreasonable. As a consequence, the history and pedigrees produced in Iceland should, in my opinion, not be cited as evidence in any serious historical thesis.

The French, Norman, Saxon and Irish chronicles must be judged each on their own merits, but by and large they support each other. Some of their authors have been accurate and careful; others have given imagination too much freedom. Those who have worked under economic and political pressure represent a special category. The truth of their statements should sometimes be read between the lines.

The chronicles of Richerus, Dudo de Saint-Quentin, and William of Jumièges, founded on contemporary evidence, local tradition and information obtained in court circles in Normandy, France and England must be treated with great reverence. Only if firm evidence to the contrary can be found, should a particular event be discounted.

Appendix V

Genealogy VI – Montgomery

There is a difference between what I wrote in *The Montgomery Millennium* and this genealogy as follows:

In *MM* I called Ragnor Gormsson – Roger de Montgomery. This was technically incorrect. The Latin chronicles of the Edict de Pitres call him Rogerius Gomerici or Gomerici or Rogerius Comes Exmesis. BG has called him Gomeric, but he would have thought of himself as Ragnor Gormsson.

I have added a Roger in between William and Hugh. William died circa 985 and Hugh died in 1050. I think it unlikely that a son would have died 65 years after his father during those times. A Roger de Montgomery is known to have died in France somewhere between 1020-40. I have made a presumption that he was Hugh's father.

Lastly, I have come to the conclusion that Hugh was the father of Roger (d. 1095) and not Roger, as BG and other historians have claimed. My reasoning is as follows:

1. William of Jumièges (Vol.VIII, ch. 35) says, "Rogerius Comes, filius Hugonis de Monte Gomerici …..natus est ex quadam neptium Gunnoris comitissae, scilicet ex Jocelina filia Weviae." Robert of Caen gives the same pedigree.

2. Ives, Bishop of Chartres, in a letter to Henry I says, "Gonnora et Senfria sorores fuerent…. ex Senfria excivit Joscelina, ex Joscelina, Rogerius de Monte Gummeri, ex Rogerio, Mabilia soror Roberti Bellimensis" (Migne, Patrologia latina, CLXII, 261). The great Bishops of the time had an obligation to record the pedigrees of noble families, because of the Church's rules on consanguinity. We can be fairly certain therefore that both the number of generations and pedigree are correct.

3. There may be some argument as to which sister married Turolf, but none as to who married Hugh – namely Jo(s)celina.

4. The problem has been that in the 3rd Charter of Troarn, Roger, Earl of Shrewsbury says, "Ego Rogerius, ex Normannis Normannus, magni autem Rogerii filius." (Cart. de Troarn, fol. I) All historians

and BG have taken this to mean that Roger's father was also called Roger.

5. Why would he put a "Norman of Normans"? I suggest that this might be read as – I Roger, a Norman of Viking descent (*In Latin generally they were referred to as Northmen*). I would like to suggest further that magni is the adjective attached to *Rogerii*, therefore, in translation it would read: "I Roger, a Norman of Viking descent and furthermore, a son of Roger the Great." Now Roger the Great or Roger Magnus is a well-established historical figure and was the first to call himself Roger de Montgomery and therefore, *filius* here, as in several other documents mentioned before, must be taken to mean descendant.

Appendix VI

Genealogy I
Dynasty of Ulvungar
House of Lothbrook (Or Brocus)

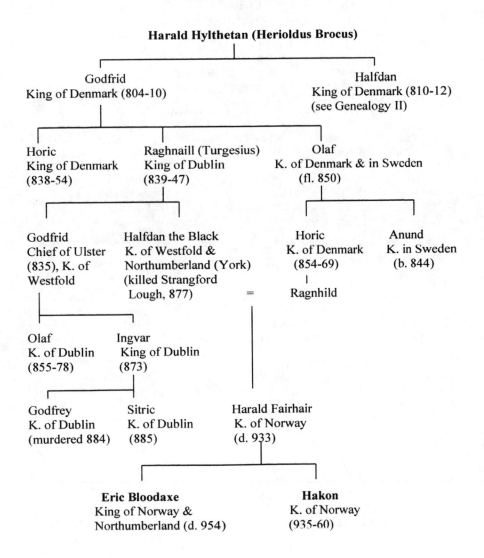

Appendix VII

Genealogy II
Dynasty of Ulvungar

House of Lothbrook (Descent from Halfdan – See Genealogy I)

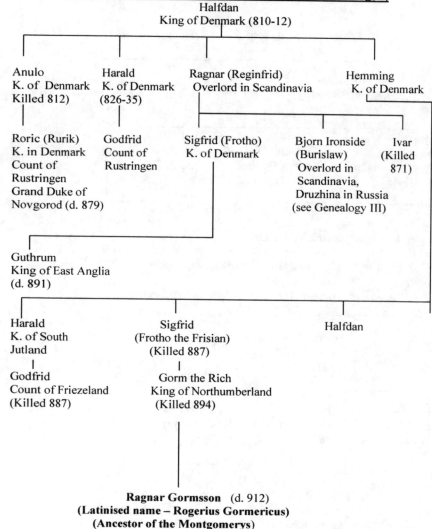

Halfdan
King of Denmark (810-12)

Anulo
K. of Denmark
Killed 812)

Harald
K. of Denmark
(826-35)

Ragnar (Reginfrid)
Overlord in Scandinavia

Hemming
K. of Denmark

Roric (Rurik)
K. in Denmark
Count of
Rustringen
Grand Duke of
Novgorod (d. 879)

Godfrid
Count of
Rustringen

Sigfrid (Frotho)
K. of Denmark

Bjorn Ironside
(Burislaw)
Overlord in
Scandinavia,
Druzhina in Russia
(see Genealogy III)

Ivar
(Killed
871)

Guthrum
King of East Anglia
(d. 891)

Harald
K. of South
Jutland

Sigfrid
(Frotho the Frisian)
(Killed 887)

Halfdan

Godfrid
Count of Friezeland
(Killed 887)

Gorm the Rich
King of Northumberland
(Killed 894)

Ragnar Gormsson (d. 912)
(Latinised name – Rogerius Gormericus)
(Ancestor of the Montgomerys)

148

Appendix VIII

Genealogy III

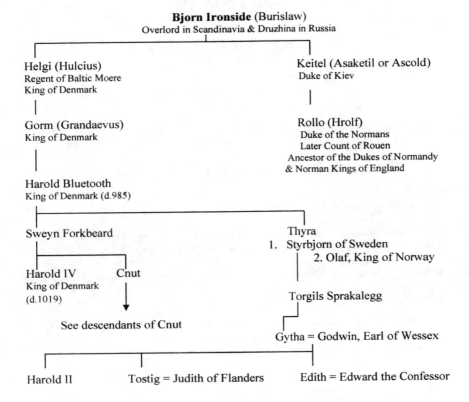

Bjorn Ironside (Burislaw)
Overlord in Scandinavia & Druzhina in Russia

Helgi (Hulcius)
Regent of Baltic Moere
King of Denmark

Keitel (Asaketil or Ascold)
Duke of Kiev

Gorm (Grandaevus)
King of Denmark

Rollo (Hrolf)
Duke of the Normans
Later Count of Rouen
Ancestor of the Dukes of Normandy
& Norman Kings of England

Harold Bluetooth
King of Denmark (d.985)

Sweyn Forkbeard

Thyra
1. Styrbjorn of Sweden
2. Olaf, King of Norway

Harold IV   Cnut
King of Denmark
(d.1019)

Torgils Sprakalegg

See descendants of Cnut

Gytha = Godwin, Earl of Wessex

Harold II   Tostig = Judith of Flanders   Edith = Edward the Confessor

This makes Rollo the third cousin once removed and slightly older of Ragnar Gormsson – see Genealogy II. It also shows that Harold was, via his mother, a member of the Ulvungar dynasty.

149

Appendix IX

Hrolf the Ganger (d/c.928)
(Rollo, Count of Rouen)

= (a) Poppa
(dau. Berenger of Bayeaux)

=(b) Gizelle
(dau. Charles, King of France)

William "Longsword" (d.942)
= (a) Espriota

(b) Leutgarda
(dau. Herbert II of Vermandois)

Richard I (d.995)
=   (a) Emma (dau. Hugh, The Great of Paris)
    (b) Gunnora of Denmark

Richard II	Robert	Malger	Hedwige	Emma	Matilda
=	(Count of	(Count of	=	=	=
(a) Judith	Evreux)	Mortain &	(Geoffrey, C.	1. Aethelred	(Eudes, C. of
of Brittany		Corbeil*)	of Brittany)	2. Cnut	Blois &
Dreux)					

(b) Papia: —————————————————————————

Richard III	Robert	Alice	Eleanor	Haduisa
	=	=	=	=
	(a) Estrith,	Renault	Baldwin	Count of
	(half-sister	Count of	Count of	Rennes
	of Cnut)	Burgundy	Flanders	
Nicholas (Priest)				

≈ (b) Herleve

Adilisa
=
Stephen II
C. of Blois &
Dreux

William
Count of
Arques

Mauger

Archbishop
of Rouen

William I	**Daughter**

= Matilda of Flanders

Appendix X

*Genealogy V
Ulvungar Dynasty

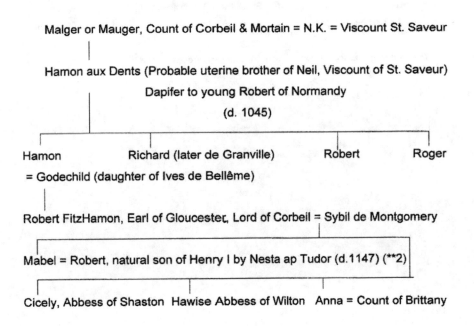

Malger or Mauger, Count of Corbeil & Mortain = N.K. = Viscount St. Saveur

Hamon aux Dents (Probable uterine brother of Neil, Viscount of St. Saveur)

Dapifer to young Robert of Normandy

(d. 1045)

Hamon   Richard (later de Granville)   Robert   Roger

= Godechild (daughter of Ives de Bellême)

Robert FitzHamon, Earl of Gloucester, Lord of Corbeil = Sybil de Montgomery

Mabel = Robert, natural son of Henry I by Nesta ap Tudor (d.1147) (**2)

Cicely, Abbess of Shaston Hawise Abbess of Wilton Anna = Count of Brittany

```
                    **2 Mabel = Robert, (Earl of Gloucester in Jus Uxore)
        |─────────────────────|───────────────|───────|──────|──────|
  William (d. 1173)   Richard, Lord of Cruelli  Robert  Roger  Philip   Maud
  = Hawise            = (Dau. Lord of St. Clare & Villersfossard )        = Ranulf
  (dau. Robert Earl of Leicester)                                    Earl of Chester
```

The above genealogy is taken from transcripts of documents found at Wardour Castle and now in the Arundel Collection.

Appendix XI

Genealogy VI
Dynasty of Ulvunger
Montgomery

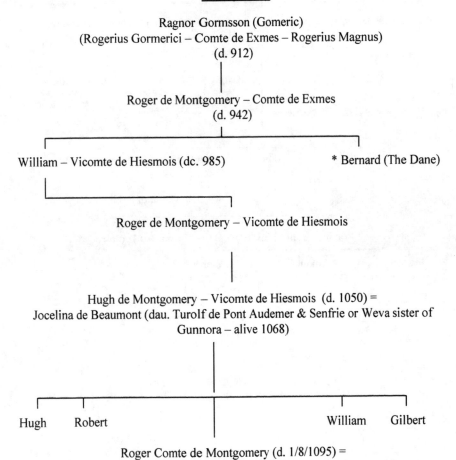

Ragnor Gormsson (Gomeric)
(Rogerius Gormerici – Comte de Exmes – Rogerius Magnus)
(d. 912)

Roger de Montgomery – Comte de Exmes
(d. 942)

William – Vicomte de Hiesmois (dc. 985)   * Bernard (The Dane)

Roger de Montgomery – Vicomte de Hiesmois

Hugh de Montgomery – Vicomte de Hiesmois (d. 1050) =
Jocelina de Beaumont (dau. Turolf de Pont Audemer & Senfrie or Weva sister of
Gunnora – alive 1068)

Hugh   Robert   William   Gilbert

Roger Comte de Montgomery (d. 1/8/1095) =
Mabel de Bellême

* Could be brother or uncle of William

Appendix XII

DESCENT FROM CHARLEMAGNE

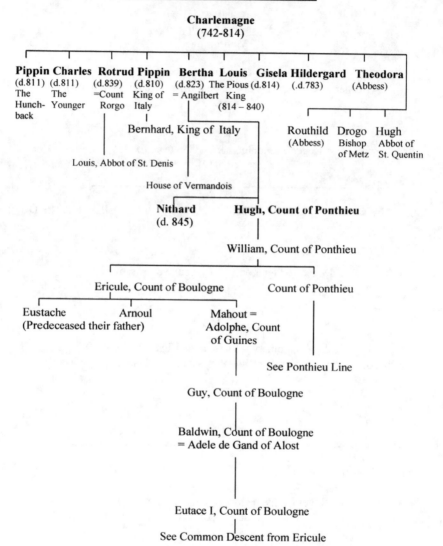

Charlemagne
(742-814)

Pippin	**Charles**	**Rotrud**	**Pippin**	**Bertha**	**Louis**	**Gisela**	**Hildergard**	**Theodora**
(d.811)	(d.811)	(d.839)	(d.810)	(d.823)	The Pious (d.814)	(.d.783)		(Abbess)
The	The	=Count	King of	= Angilbert	King			
Hunch-	Younger	Rorgo	Italy		(814 – 840)			
back								

Bernhard, King of Italy

Routhild   Drogo   Hugh
(Abbess)   Bishop   Abbot of
     of Metz   St. Quentin

Louis, Abbot of St. Denis

House of Vermandois

Nithard   **Hugh, Count of Ponthieu**
(d. 845)

William, Count of Ponthieu

Ericule, Count of Boulogne   Count of Ponthieu

Eustache   Arnoul   Mahout =
(Predeceased their father)   Adolphe, Count
     of Guines

See Ponthieu Line

Guy, Count of Boulogne

Baldwin, Count of Boulogne
= Adele de Gand of Alost

Eutace I, Count of Boulogne

See Common Descent from Ericule

Ref: Platts, B. op. cit. Vol. I, p. 38; Also Montgomery, H. op. cit. pp.2 & 3; Also Karl der Grosse; Also McKitterick, R. (1983) – *The Frankish Kingdoms under the Carolingians,* 781-987, pp. 349-367, Longman Group, Essex, UK.

Appendix XIII

Ericule, Count of Boulogne
(965, under Lothair – Descent from Charlemagne via Bertha & Angilbert)
Eustace I, Count of Boulogne
= Matilda of Louvain *

```
                    Eustace II, Count of Boulogne =        Ida = Baldwin
           (a) Godgifu (dau. of Aethelred II & Emma of Normandy)    of Le Bourg
    (b) Ida of Lorraine (dau. of Godfrey, Duke of Lower Lorraine & Doda of the line of
                                  Charlemagne)
```

Eustace III	Godfrey of	Baldwin
= Mary of Scotland	Bouillon (b.c. 1060)	Count of Edessa
(dau. Malcolm III &	Duke of Lower Lorraine	later King of
Margaret)	Prince of Jerusalem & Defender	Jerusalem
	of the Holy Sepulcre	= (a) Godvere of
		Tosny **
Matilda = Stephen		(b) dau. of Thatoul
C. de Blois		(c) Adelaide, Countess
		of Sicily

* Adela of Louvain was the 1st. wife of Henry I of England. His 2nd wife was
Matilda, sister of Mary of Scotland.
**William FitzOsborn, cousin of William the Conqueror, had married Aeliz de Tosny
  (her Aunt?).

COMMON DESCENT FROM

Robert Fitz-Hamon
Seigneur, later Count of Corbeil
= Sibil (dau. of Roger de Montgomery) *

Bouchard of Montlhery & Corbeil
= Adelaide of Crecy

Melisende	Alice (or Adela)	Isabella
= Hugh I of Rethel	= Everard of Le Puiset	= Joscelin de
(son of Baldwin of Le Bourg	(son of Ebrard de Le Puiset	Courtenay
Count of Rethel - cousin of	whose daughter Adeliza was	
Godfrey & Baldwin)	2nd wife of Roger de Montgomery)	

Notes on Descent from Ericule:
Ericule had two sons, Arnoul and Eustache, and a daughter Mahaut. His two sons
predeceased him and his daughter's husband Adolphe, Count of Guines, succeeded in
his wife's name. Their son Guy then became Count of Boulogne, to be suceeded by his
son Baldwin, who married Adele de Gand, sister of the Lord of Alost. Baldwin's son
was Eustace I. (See Platts, B. (1985) – *Scottish Hazard* Vol. I p. 26, Procter Press,
London.)
* See Ponthieu line from Charlemagne.

The Bellême Dynasty

Yves de Bellême (d. 940)
Grand Master of Crossbowmen
Governor of Creil
= Godehilde (d. after 1005)
(4 x great grandaughter of Chlothar IV)

Guilluime I (1005-1031)
Prince & Seigneur of Bellême & Alençon
(Confidant of Robert the Pious)
= Mathilde

Robert I de Bellême
(1031-1033)
(Killed Chateau de Ballon)

Guilluime II de Talvas (or Talvais)
(1033-1053)
"Prince of Bellême"

=(a) Hildeburge
=(b) Daughter of Raoul de Beaumont

Mabile (Daughter of Guilluime II)
(1053-1082)
(Killed Chateau de Bures-sur-Dives)
= Roger de Montgomery
Vicomte d'Exmes (Hiesmois)

Robert II de Montgomery (Talvas)
Prince of Bellême
(1082-1114)
(Was dispossessed of Belleme by Henry I and died in prison after 1127)
= Agnes de Ponthieu

(Ref: The above information comes from Chahiers Percherons, Triem.
No: 51, 3rd. Trimestre 1976 – Published by the Assoc. de Amis du Perche
and found by me in the Library in the Marie de Belleme.)

There are some differences in dates regarding the death of Robert II de
Belleme.
The dates in brackets are the dates of titular possession.

Appendix XV

MONTGOMERY, COUNTS OF BELLÊME & THE LEUFROYS

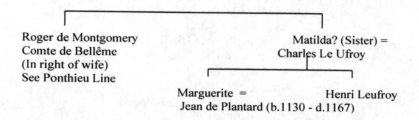

Roger de Montgomery
Comte de Bellême
(In right of wife)
See Ponthieu Line

Matilda? (Sister) =
Charles Le Ufroy

Marguerite =
Jean de Plantard (b.1130 - d.1167)

Henri Leufroy

Ref: Vicomte du Motey (1923) – *Robert II de Bellesme et son temps*, Paris.

Appendix XVI

PONTHIEU LINE FROM CHARLEMAGNE

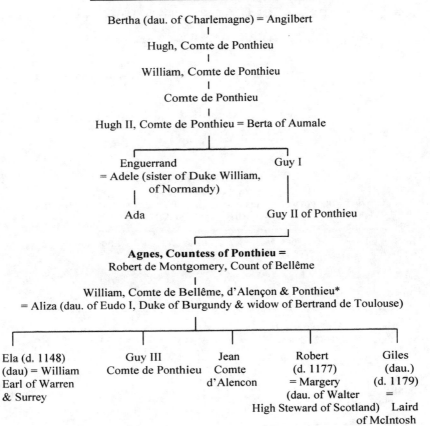

Bertha (dau. of Charlemagne) = Angilbert

Hugh, Comte de Ponthieu

William, Comte de Ponthieu

Comte de Ponthieu

Hugh II, Comte de Ponthieu = Berta of Aumale

Enguerrand
= Adele (sister of Duke William, of Normandy)

Ada

Guy I

Guy II of Ponthieu

Agnes, Countess of Ponthieu =
Robert de Montgomery, Count of Bellême

William, Comte de Bellême, d'Alençon & Ponthieu*
= Aliza (dau. of Eudo I, Duke of Burgundy & widow of Bertrand de Toulouse)

Ela (d. 1148)
(dau) = William
Earl of Warren
& Surrey

Guy III
Comte de Ponthieu

Jean
Comte
d'Alencon

Robert
(d. 1177)
= Margery
(dau. of Walter
High Steward of Scotland)

Giles
(dau.)
(d. 1179)
=
Laird
of McIntosh

* The above is shown by a letter from the Bishop of Sees when Corbeil married Sybil Montgomery because they had to obtain papal dispensation, as they were near cousins. (Original now in the Bodleian, Oxford.)

Appendix XVII

Simplified Tree of the Merovingians (447-737 AD)

MEROVEE THE ELDER, Known as Merovech
(447-487)
(Helped Roman General Aetius to defeat Attila the Hun
at Battle of Catalaunian Plains, 451 AD)

Childeric I
(b.436)
King of Tournai
(481-511)

Clovis I
= Clotilda of Burgundy
(Clovis is thought to have become a Christian together with 3000 soldiers
at Rheims in 496 AD)

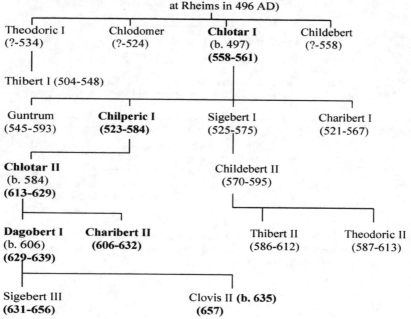

Theodoric I (?-534)   Chlodomer (?-524)   **Chlotar I** (b. 497) **(558-561)**   Childebert (?-558)

Thibert I (504-548)

Guntrum (545-593)   **Chilperic I (523-584)**   Sigebert I (525-575)   Charibert I (521-567)

Chlotar II (b. 584) **(613-629)**   Childebert II (570-595)

Dagobert I (b. 606) **(629-639)**   **Charibert II (606-632)**   Thibert II (586-612)   Theodoric II (587-613)

Sigebert III **(631-656)**   Clovis II **(b. 635)** **(657)**

160

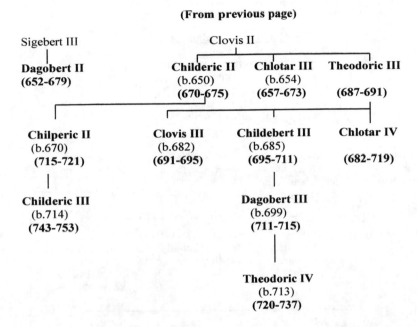

(From previous page)

Sigebert III

Clovis II

Dagobert II
(652-679)

Childeric II
(b.650)
(670-675)

Chlotar III
(b.654)
(657-673)

Theodoric III

(687-691)

Chilperic II
(b.670)
(715-721)

Clovis III
(b.682)
(691-695)

Childebert III
(b.685)
(695-711)

Chlotar IV

(682-719)

Childeric III
(b.714)
(743-753)

Dagobert III
(b.699)
(711-715)

Theodoric IV
(b.713)
(720-737)

Ref: Wenzler, C. (1995) – *The Kings of France*, p. 3, Editions Ouest-France, Rennes, France, Trans. Angela Moyon

Clovis I died in 511 and his kingdom divided by his sons, who annexed Burgundy in 534 AD and Provence in 537 AD.

After the deaths of his brothers, Chlotar I became King of Regnum Francorum in 558, but upon his death his kingdom was once again divided. Charibert I became King of Paris, Guntrum became King of Burgundy, Sigebert of Austrasia and Chilperic I of Soissons.

Dagobert I re-established most of the kingdom but once again, his sons' divisions caused problems. Sigebert II was King of Austrasia and Clovis II King of Burgundy & Neustria.

The last Merovingian monarch, Childeric II, was confined to a monastery by Pepin the Short who, with the connivance of Pope Zacharias, then seized the throne.

Appendix XVIII

The Makhirs of Septimania

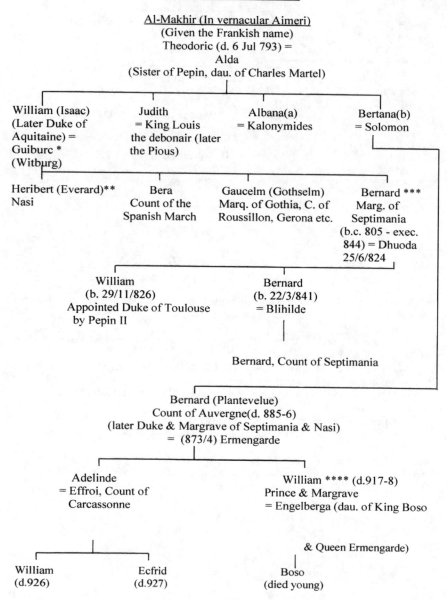

Al-Makhir (In vernacular Aimeri)
(Given the Frankish name)
Theodoric (d. 6 Jul 793) =
Alda
(Sister of Pepin, dau. of Charles Martel)

William (Isaac)
(Later Duke of
Aquitaine) =
Guiburc *
(Witburg)

Judith
= King Louis
the debonair (later
the Pious)

Albana(a)
= Kalonymides

Bertana(b)
= Solomon

Heribert (Everard)**
Nasi

Bera
Count of the
Spanish March

Gaucelm (Gothselm)
Marq. of Gothia, C. of
Roussillon, Gerona etc.

Bernard ***
Marg. of
Septimania
(b.c. 805 - exec.
844) = Dhuoda
25/6/824

William
(b. 29/11/826)
Appointed Duke of Toulouse
by Pepin II

Bernard
(b. 22/3/841)
= Blihilde

Bernard, Count of Septimania

Bernard (Plantevelue)
Count of Auvergne(d. 885-6)
(later Duke & Margrave of Septimania & Nasi)
= (873/4) Ermengarde

Adelinde
= Effroi, Count of
Carcassonne

William **** (d.917-8)
Prince & Margrave
= Engelberga (dau. of King Boso

& Queen Ermengarde)

William
(d.926)

Ecfrid
(d.927)

Boso
(died young)

Notes:

I produced the above genealogical tree from the information in Professor Arthur Zuckerman's book, A Jewish Princedom in Feudal France 768-900, published by Columbia University Press, New York & London.

(a) & (b) It is not clear from the literature as to whether Bertrana married Solomon and Albana married the Kalomides, or vice versa. It simply says "daughter of," without indicating her name.

*   A non-Christian from beyond the sea.

**   Opposed Agobard and was blinded by Lothar.

***   Count of Barcelona, later Camerarius (Chamberlain) to Louis and protector of infant Charles. Nasi, after the blinding of Heribert. Most important person after the Emperor. Septimania called a "Kingdom" at this time. Cousin of Eudo of Orleans.

**** William founded an institution of Jewish learning in what became the Abbey of Cluny. After his death he was christianised by the Church and became known as William the Pious.

Bernard Plantevelue was known as "Hairy Foot."

With the end of the line of the original Makhirs, the collateral branch of the Kalonymides of Lucca were asked in 917 by King Charles (893-923) to come to the Narbonne as Nasis. The first of this line was known in Hebrew as Rabbi Moses the Elder; his son's cognomen was "En-Kalonymos." This line continued at least until the

14th Century. In 1246 we find a Charter signed in Hebrew (Moumet Judeu d'Nerpo) and sealed with the Seal of the Lion Rampant of the House of Judah and a six-pointed star and, in 1307-8, we find references to "Momet Tauros – King of the Jews."

The name "Makhir," or its Frankish form "Aimeri," is not really a proper name but more of a title, indicating someone who is the spiritual as well as civil and often military head of the Jewish people in that area, particularly in the Aquitaine region where many members of the nobility married into this family or gave their daughters in marriage to the Makhirs. It is very likely also, that several noble families converted to Judaism or, at the very least, accepted it. For example, in the Diet of Pitres in 864, Pippin II of Aquitaine was accused of apostasy to paganism (of the Norsemen?). It seems to me more likely that he became a Jew. Thus, Theodoric was Al-Makhir as was William (Isaac Al-Makhir) and Heribert would have Al-Makhir before being blinded, at which point his brother Bernard became Al-Makhir. Equally, when Bernard (Plantevelue) became the Nasi he would have become Al_Makhir or Aimeri, as would his son Bernard, and when Rabbi Moses the Elder was asked to become Nasi by Charles, he would have been known as "Aimeri" in the vernacular. We can say, therefore, with a fair degree of certainty that Aimeri de Thouars was clearly a descendent of the Makhirs and leader of his people in that area of Aquitaine (see Zuckerman, A. op.cit. p. 367).

Appendix XIX

The Odonic Line of Wessex

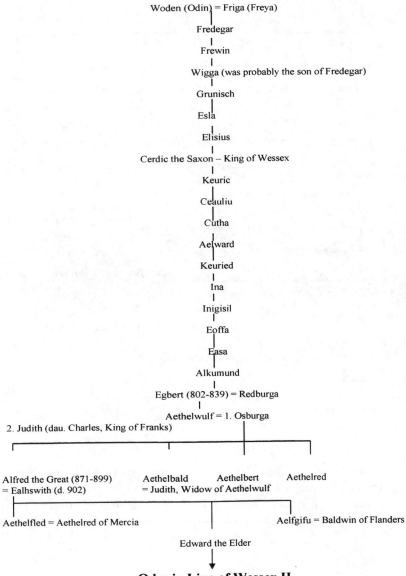

Woden (Odin) = Friga (Freya)

Fredegar

Frewin

Wigga (was probably the son of Fredegar)

Grunisch

Esla

Elisius

Cerdic the Saxon – King of Wessex

Keuric

Ceauliu

Cutha

Aelward

Keuried

Ina

Inigisil

Eoffa

Easa

Alkumund

Egbert (802-839) = Redburga

Aethelwulf = 1. Osburga

2. Judith (dau. Charles, King of Franks)

Alfred the Great (871-899)   Aethelbald   Aethelbert   Aethelred
= Ealhswith (d. 902)   = Judith, Widow of Aethelwulf

Aethelfled = Aethelred of Mercia   Aelfgifu = Baldwin of Flanders

Edward the Elder

Odonic Line of Wessex II

Odonic Line of Wessex II

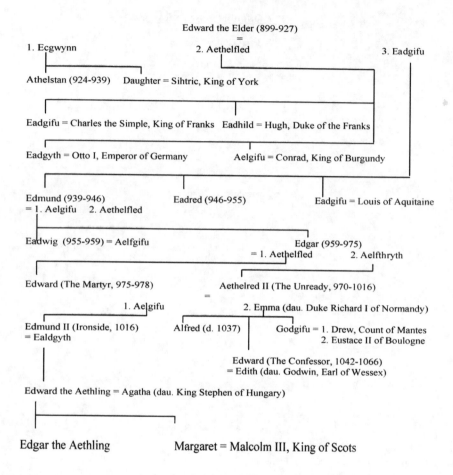

Edward the Elder (899-927)
=

1. Ecgwynn   2. Aethelfled   3. Eadgifu

Athelstan (924-939)   Daughter = Sihtric, King of York

Eadgifu = Charles the Simple, King of Franks Eadhild = Hugh, Duke of the Franks

Eadgyth = Otto I, Emperor of Germany   Aelgifu = Conrad, King of Burgundy

Edmund (939-946)   Eadred (946-955)   Eadgifu = Louis of Aquitaine
= 1. Aelgifu   2. Aethelfled

Eadwig (955-959) = Aelfgifu   Edgar (959-975)
                                     = 1. Aethelfled   2. Aelfthryth

Edward (The Martyr, 975-978)   Aethelred II (The Unready, 970-1016)
                                      =
            1. Aelgifu   2. Emma (dau. Duke Richard I of Normandy)
Edmund II (Ironside, 1016)   Alfred (d. 1037)   Godgifu = 1. Drew, Count of Mantes
= Ealdgyth   2. Eustace II of Boulogne

                                      Edward (The Confessor, 1042-1066)
                                      = Edith (dau. Godwin, Earl of Wessex)

Edward the Aethling = Agatha (dau. King Stephen of Hungary)

Edgar the Aethling   Margaret = Malcolm III, King of Scots

I compiled the above from the Wessex King Lists in the Royal Collection and the Oxford History of the British Monarchy and Florence of Worcester. Some versions of the King Lists include "Baeldaeg and Brond" between "Woden and Fredegar."

Appendix XX

Y Chromosome Census of the British Isles

A recent publication in the Journal of Current Biology has mapped out the distribution of various Y chromosome haplotypes in order to establish the impact of invading groups on the indigenous population. In particular, these were benchmarked against known Basque, Germanic/Danish and Norwegian haplotypes.

The results show that the main invading forces from Scandinavia were R1a1, I & I1b2 and a small number of J2. Whilst as there were no J2s from Norway, there were a considerable number of J2s either from Germany or more probably Denmark, but because Denmark is basically a peninsular sticking out of north Germany, the study was unable to distinguish between the north German and Danish haplotypes.

As the House of Brocus was a Danish line, it would seem to show that it could well have been J2. However, the study makes the assumption that these groups derive from the Palaeolithic period. Whilst this is certainly possible, the theory that they derive from the early Bronze Age cannot be ruled out.

Ref: Capelli, C., Redhead, N. et al (2003) – A Y Chromosome Census of the British Isles, Journal of Current Biology, Vol. 13 (May 27), pp. 979-984, Elsevier Science, Ltd.

REFERENCES, SOURCES & FURTHER READING

www.art.man.ac.uj/ARTHIST/Estates/Hamilton.htm

www.ancientroute.com/empire/edom.htm

http://www.bible.ca/history/fathers/ANF-08/anf08-66.htm

http://i-cias.com/e.o/nabateans.htm

http://www.earlybritishkingdoms.com/articles/josanc.html

http://www.domainofman.com/book/sup5.html

http://fmg.ac/Projects/MedLands/TOULOUSE.htm

http://www.touregypt.net/featurestories/set.htm

Abecassis, A. & Eisenberg, J. (1978) – A Bible Ouverte, Albin Michel, Paris.

Abdias Manuscript, Norris Collection, USA.

Ackroyd, P. (2001) – London, Vintage Books.

Acts of Thomas, New Testament Apocrypha.

Al-Makkari, A. ibn M. (1968) – History of the Mohammedan Dynasties in Spain, Editiones Espagnoles, Spain.

Albert of Aix (c. 1100) – Liber Christianae Expeditionis pro Ereptione Emundatione et Restitutione Sanctae Hierosolymitanae Ecclesiae, vols. I-III.

Albright, W. F. (1942) – King Joiachim in Exile, The Biblical Archaeologist, UK.

Amatus of Montecassino – Storia de'Normanni, ed. Bartholomaeis, (trans. J. J. Norwich).

Annals of the Kingdom of Ireland by the Four Masters, (trans. O'Donovan – 1887-1901), Dublin.

Ante-Nicene Fathers, Vols. I-VIII, von Tischendorf Collection, Strathclyde University Library.

Army Essays (2007) – The Wends 580-1218 AD, III-1a, DBA Resources.

Ashley, M. (1973) – The Life and Times of William I, Weidenfeld & Nicholson, UK.

Baigent, M. (2006) – The Jesus Papers, Harper-Element.

Bain, R. (1938) – The Clans and Tartans of Scotland, (7th edition), W. Collins & Sons.

Baker, J. H. (1981) – An Introduction to English Legal History, 2nd Edition, Butterworth & Co. London.

Barber, R. (1970) – The Knight and Chivalry, Longman, London.

Barber, R. (1978) – Edward, Prince of Wales and Aquitaine, Boydell Press.

Bartlett, R. (2000) – England under the Norman and Angevin Kings 1075-1225, Clarendon Press, UK.

Bauer, W. (1934) (English Edition – 1971) – Orthodoxy and Heresy in Earliest Christianity.

Bayeaux Tapestry, from photographs taken by Mr. E. Barrow.

Begg, E. (2000) – The Cult of the Black Madonna.

Bennett, M. (1988) – Wace and Warfare, Anglo-Norman Studies.

Bernard of Clairvaux (1129) – De Laude Novae Militae, Paris.

Bethany, House of (c.1420) – Liber Burgundiorum, Brussels (Private Collection).

Blondel, S. (1978) – The Varangians of Byzantium, (trans. Benedikz, B. S.), Cambridge.

Bradbury, J. (1998) – The Battle of Hastings, Sutton Publishing Ltd. UK.

Brown, D. (2000) – Ring Gives Clue to Last Romans, Journal of the Council of British Archaeology.

Brown, R. A. (1984) – The Normans, Boydell Press.

Campbell, J. (2000) – The Anglo-Saxon State, Hambledon & London, UK.

Canon, J. & Griffiths, R. (1988) – Oxford History of the British Monarchy, Oxford University Press.

Castledon, R. (1994) – World History, A Chronological Dictionary of Dates, Paragon, UK.

Chahiers Percherons, (1976) – No. 51, Assoc. de Amis du Perche, France.

Chron. Fontaneille, Library in Perche, France.

Clough, S. B. & Cole, C.W. (1967) – Economic History of Europe, Heath & Co. Boston.

Codex Petropolitanus, Liber Historiae Francorum.

Codex Theodosianus (315) – Edition Mommsen & Meyer.

Collection Cornelius Harmsfort, (1546-1627), Danish State Archives.

Comnena, A. (c. 1100) – Alexiad (ed. B. Leib) Vols I-III, Collection Byzantine de l'Association Guillaume Budé, Paris (1937-1945).

Crouch, D. (2002) – The Normans, Hambledon & London, UK.

Daud, ibn A. (1160-1161) – Sefer Seder haKabbalah, Adler's Manuscript No. 2237, Jewish Theological Seminary of America, USA.

David, C. W. (1920) – Robert Curthose, Harvard University Press.

Davis, N. (1999) – The Isles: A History, Macmillan, London, UK.

Dennys, R. (1987) – Our Royal Sovereigns, Danbury, UK.

Den Store Danske Encyklopaedi (1998).

De Voraign, Jacobus (1275) – Aurea Legenda, Edited by Ellis, F. S. (1900), Temple Classics, UK.

Dimont, M. J. (1962) – Jews, God & History, Signet Books, London, UK.

Domesday Book, (1985) Edition Hutchinson Ltd.

Drower, Lady E. S. (1937) – The Mandeans of Iraq and Iran, Oxford. Univ. Press.

Duane, O. B. (1997) – Chivalry, Brockhampton Press, UK.

Dudo of St. Quentin (c. 1025) – De moribus et actis primorum Normanniae Ducum (ed. J. Lair 1865), Caen.

Eisenmann, R & Wise, M. (1992) – The Dead Sea Scrolls Uncovered, Penguin Books.

Eisenmann, R. (1977) – James the Brother of Jesus, Viking Penguin.

Encyclopaedia Britannica, 11th Edition.

Eusebius, (1981) – History of the Church from Christ to Constantine, (translated by G. A. Williamson), Harmondsworth. Also (1998 reprint), Hendrickson Publishers Inc., MA.

Eusebius of Caesarea, (c. 325 AD) – Epistle of Jesus Christ to Abgarus, King of Edessa, Harmondsworth.

Florence of Worchester, Manuscript published in 1854 by Henry Bohn, partly translated by Thomas Forrester, Djursholm, Sweden.

Ford, D. N. (2006) – Early British Kingdoms, Articles josanc.

Fulcher of Chartres – Gesta Francorum Iherusalem Peregrinantium, (ed. Hagenmeyer 1913), Heidelberg.

Gardiner, G. (2000) – The Bloodline of the Holy Grail.

Garrett, G. (1988) – Conquered England 1066-1215, Oxford Illustrated History of Medieval Europe, UK.

Gesta Danorum, Books 1-10, Danish State Archives.

Gillingham, J. (1998) – The Normans in the Lives of the Kings and Queens of England, Weidenfeld and Nicholson Ltd. UK.

Glueck, N. (1965) – Deities and Dolphins: The Story of the Nabataeans, New York.

Guy de Amiens, (c.1100) – Carmen de Hastingae Proelio.

Hallam, E. (Editor) (1986) – The Plantagenet Chronicles, Phoebe Philips & Macmillan Publishers.

Hardrada, Harald – The Gamanvisur, Skaldic Verses, Royal Library Sweden.

Harris, R. Rt. Rev. (1993) – Art and Beauty of God, Mowbray, London.

Heimskringla, Sweden.

Hicks, C. (1998) – England in the 11th Century, Stamford Press, USA.

Hill, R. (ed.) (1962) – Gesta Francorum, Nelson Medieval Texts, London.

James, E. (1988) – The Northern World in the Dark Ages 400-900, Oxford Illustrated History of Medieval Europe, UK.

James, M. R. (ed.) (1953) – The Apocryphal New Testament, Clarendon Press, UK.

Jerlow, L. G. (ed.) (1968) – Ordo Niderosiensis Ecclesiae, Oslo.

Jómsvíkingadrápa, Sweden.

Jómsvíkinga saga, Sweden.

Josephus (1981) – The Jewish War (trans. G. A. Williamson). Also Antiquities of the Jews.

Kelly's Handbook to the Titled, Landed and Official Classes, various years.

Kjeilen, T. (2006) – LexiOrient – Nabateans.

Kraeling, C. H. (1951) – John the Baptist, Schribner's Sons, London.

Lair, J. (1885) – Introductory notes to Dudon de Saint-Quentian, Mémoires de la Société de Antiquitaires de Normandie.

Le Loup, J-Y. (Trans.) (2003) – The Gospel of Philip, Inner Traditions, USA.

Le Loup, J-Y. (Trans.) (2002) – The Gospel of Mary Magdalene, Inner Traditions, USA.

Le Loup, J-Y. (Trans.) (2005) – The Gospel of Thomas, Inner Traditions, USA.

Levi, I. (1895) – L'origine davidique de Hillel, Revue des études juives, France.

Liber Hymnorum – MSS. E. 4,2; Trinity College, Dublin.

Lopes, A. (1997) – The Popes, Futura Edizioni, Roma.

Loud, G. A. (1981) – Gens Normannorum, Journal of Anglo-Saxon Studies, UK.

Maclagan, M. & Louda, J. (1999) – Lines of Succession, Little, Brown & Co.

MacQuitty, W. (1976) – The Island of Isis, Book Club Associates, London.

Malaterra, Gaufridus (c. 1098) – Historia Sicula, ed. Migne, Patrologia Latina.

Mander, A & R. (2002) – The Black Madonna, Published privately.

Martin, M. (1981) – The Decline and Fall of the Roman Church, G. P. Putnam's Sons, New York.

McFarlan, D. M. (2005) – Dictionary of the Bible, Geddess & Grosset.

McKitterick, R. (1983) – The Frankish Kingdoms under the Carolingians, Longman, UK.

McLynn, F. (1995) – 1066, The Year of the Three Battles, Jonathon Cape, London, UK.

Medieval Source Book, Fordham University Center for Medieval Studies.

Montgomery, B. G. (1968) – Ancient Migrations and Royal Houses, Mitre Press, UK.

Montgomery, H. (2002) – Montgomery Millennium, Megatrend, Belgrade.

Montgomery, H. (2006) – The God-Kings of Europe, The Book Tree, San Diego, California.

Montgomery, H. (2007) – The God-Kings of England, Temple Publications, UK.

Morkot, R. G. (2000) – The Black Pharaohs, Rubicon Press.

Manuscript M/s. 481.51-100 – Yale University Collection of Rare Books and Manuscripts.

Munch, P. A. (1810-1863) – Der Norske Folks Historie, Sweden.

Muhammed, Abu J. (1972) – Tasfir-Ibn-i-Jarir at Tabri, Vols I-III, Kubr-ul-Mar Press Cairo.

Norwich, J. J. – Byzantium, Penguin Books.

Odericus Vitalis, Origine de la Normandie, Paris edition, 1920.

Odericus Vitalis, Historia Ecclesiastica, Macmillan.

Oleson, T. J. (1955) – The Witanagemot in the Reign of Edward the Confessor, English Historical Review (EHR), London, UK.

Olaf Tryggvasson's Saga, Sweden.

Oleson, T. J. (1953) – Edward the Confessor's Promise of the Throne to Duke William of Normandy, HER.

Oman, Sir Charles, (1991 Edition) – History of the Art of War in the Middle Ages, Vols. I, II, Greenhill Books.

Pagels, E. & King, K. L. (2007) – Reading Judas, Allen Lane.

Payne, R. (1984) – The Dream and the Tomb, Penguin.

Patai, R. (1990) – The Hebrew Goddess, Detroit.

Peterborough Chronicler, (c. 1070).

Platts, B. (1985) – Scottish Hazard, Vols. I & II, Proctor Press.

Pope, C. N. (2005) – Herodian Identities of the New Testament Characters, domainofman.com.

Powicke, Sir F. M. & Fryde, E. B. (1961) – Handbook of British Chronology, 2nd Edition, Royal Historical Society.

Poynder, M. – Mary Magdalene – awaiting publication.

Public Record Office M/s 101/387/25 m. 27.

Pükert, W. (1953) – Aniane und Gellone, Germany.

Raymond of Aguilers, (c. 1100) – Historia Francorum qui ceperunt Jerusalem, R. H. C. Occ.; Vol. III.

Revel, J. (1918) – Historie des Normans, Paris.

Runciman, Sir S. (1951) – The History of the Crusades, Vols. I-III, Cambridge University Press.

Sawyer, B. & P. (1993) – Medieval Scandinavia from Conversion to Reformation, c. 800-1500, UK.

Schimann, J. (1951) – Samuel Hannagid, the Man, the Soldier, the Politician, Jewish Social Studies.

Schneid, H. (1973) – Marriage, Keter Books, Jerusalem.

Schorim, Ben S. (1978) – Mon frère Jésus, Editions du Seuil.

Seawright, C. (2007) – Set (Seth), God of Storms, Slayer of Apep, Equal to and Rival of Horus, featurestories/set.htm.

Series Runica Prima, Danish State Archives.

Sinclair, Dr. H. – Jesus' Family, private papers in possession of Clan Sinclair Trust.

Smith, M. (1974) – The Secret Gospel, Gollancz.

Steenstrup, J. (1882) – Normannerne, Library B. G. Montgomery, Sweden.

Stoyanov, Y. (1994) – The Hidden Tradition in Europe, Penguin.

Swanton, M. (2000) – Anglo-Saxon Chronicle, Phoenix Press.

Szekely, E. B. (1996) – The Gospel of the Essenes, Daniel & Co. UK.

Szekely, E. & Weaver, P. (1986) – The Gospel of Peace of Jesus Christ, C. Daniel & Co. Ltd. UK.

Taylor, J. – A Second Temple in Egypt, Waikato University Press.

Taylor, J. (1967) – Letters of Eleutherius to King Lucius.

The Three Fragments, M/s. in the Burgundian Library, Brussels.

Thiering, B. (1992) – Jesus the Man, BCA, London.

Turner, L. (2006) – Lectures in Egyptology, Uttoxeter and District U3A.

Wace, R. (c. 1135) – Le Roman de Rou, (ed. A. J. Holden), 3 volumes, Soc. des Anciens Texts Français (1970-1973).

Wahlberg, E. (1913) – Sur L'Origine de Rollon, France.

William of Jumierges (c. 1130) – Gesta Normannorum Ducum.

William of Malmesbury (c. 1129) – De gestis regum Anglorum.

William of Poitiers (c. 1074-1077) – Gesta Guillelmi Ducis Normannorum et Regis Anglorum.

William of Tyre, (c. 1200) – Historia – Rerum in Partibus Transmarinis Gestarum, R. H. C. Occ. IV. Also (c. 1108) – Die Latinische Fortsetzung (ed. Salloch 1934), Leipzig.

Worsac, J. (1863) – Den danske Erobring af England og Nomanniet, Denmark.

Yeatman, J. P. (1882) – History of the House of Arundel, Mitchell & Hughes.

Zosima, Historia – Private Copy.

Zuckerman, A. J. (1972) – A Jewish Princedom in Feudal France 768-900, Columbia University Press, USA.

CPSIA information can be obtained at www.ICGtesting.com
Printed in the USA
LVOW051607190613

339337LV00005B/748/P